'ħ'

OLIVER TWIST

Adapted in Twenty-Four Scenes
with Several Songs and Tableaux

by Neil Bartlett

OBERON BOOKS
LONDON

This adaptation first published in 2004 by Oberon Books Ltd.
(incorporating Absolute Classics)
521 Caledonian Road, London N7 9RH
Tel: 020 7607 3637 / Fax: 020 7607 3629
e-mail: oberon.books@btinternet.com
www.oberonbooks.com

A catalogue record for this book is available from the British
Library.

ISBN: 1 84002 427 5

Printed in Great Britain by Antony Rowe Ltd, Chippenham.

Contents

LYRIC HAMMERSMITH
A LONDON ORIGINAL

Hidden away behind a concrete facade on a busy London high street, the Lyric has always been one of the most surprising theatres in London.

The spring 2004 season, which opens with the Lyric's production of Oliver Twist, fills the main stage with extraordinary images, powerful stories and live music both strange and lovely. Following a five-week run in London, Oliver Twist then tours across the country to Guildford, Bath, Newcastle, Edinburgh, Warwick and Brighton.

Back in London, the Lyric's own productions rub creative shoulders with visitors including Gone to Earth by Shared Experience, the legendary Shockheaded Peter and Mexico City's extraordinary Astrid Hadad. Meanwhile, in the Lyric Studio, we're presenting seven new pieces from the rising generation of theatremakers.

This season, after £2.6 million of fundraising and twelve months of building work, the Lyric also declares it's new front door, rehearsal studio and education and training room, well and truly open for business. To celebrate the opening on the weekend of 3rd and 4th April twenty artists from around the country and around the world combine forces to fill every available space in the building with a continuous programme of performances, installations and happenings.

With its trademark free first nights, great value tickets and bargain Mondays, the Lyric has a reputation for working to bring the boldest and the best of contemporary theatre to as wide an audience as possible. Whether you're seeing Oliver Twist in Hammersmith, or on the road, I hope you enjoy your night out with the Lyric.

Neil Bartlett
Artistic Director

Lyric Theatre Hammersmith
King Street
London W6 0QL
Tel: 020 8741 0824
Fax: 020 8741 5965
Email: enquiries@lyric.co.uk

Registered Charity No. 278518

LYRIC COMPANY

Executive Director — Simon Mellor
Artistic Director — Neil Bartlett
General Manager — Jackie McNerney
Artistic Associates — Siobhan Bracke
Rachel Clare
Michael Morris
Alex Poots

Finance
Finance Manager — Frances Mulcahy
Finance Officer — Carolyn Braby

Administration
Administrator — Neil Morris
Assistant Producer — Ana Gillespie
Administration Assistant — Rebecca Feltham

Communications
Director of Communications — Jessica Hepburn
Development Manager — Kate Plastow
Capital Project
Development Manager — Joe Foulsham
Development Assistant — Pak Ling Wan

Marketing Manager — Louise Richards
Graphic Designer — Sara Morrissey
Senior Marketing Officer — Emily Bromfield
Marketing Officer — Damian Llambias
Marketing Assistant — Jennifer Smith

Ticket Sales Manager — Cookie Rameder
Ticket Office Supervisor — Gemma Donohue
Full-Time Ticket Office Assistants — Lib Murray, James Wilson
Part-Time Ticket Office Assistants — Becca Hartley, Gez Hebburn, Hugo Rhys, Sharon Morwood, Billie Wallace, Catherine Clissold-Jones

Education
Education and Studio Director — Claire Hicks
Education Manager — Eric Dupin
Community Drama Associate — David Baker
Education Administrator — Herta Queirazza
Education Associates — Chrissie Adesina, Sandra Agard, Belinda Earle, Jon Owen, Rebwar Rashed

Production
Production Manager — Jo Peake
Assistant Production Manager — Cara Byrne
Technical Stage Manager — Seamus Benson
Deputy Technical Stage Manager — Tom Arnold
Studio and Events Technical Manager — George Ogilvie
Chief Electrician — Tim Owen
Deputy Chief Electrician — Jane Dutton
Sound Technician — Nick Manning

Staging Dickens: Making a New Stage Version of Oliver Twist

Any new stage version of a story which the audience feels they not only know but own before the curtain even rises has to do two apparently contradictory things. It has to deliver all the famous bits (so that no-one feels short-changed), and to make the audience feel that they encountering the story anew, afresh; that they are hearing and seeing things which they either never knew or had forgotten were there. These are the twin imperatives which shaped the script printed here.

The first decision taken was that the adaptation would be made out of Dickens' original language and nothing but. With the exception of one or two short phrases necessitated by the telescoping of the novel's plot – especially that part of it which deals with the extraordinarily obscure family relationship between Mr Brownlow and Oliver – this is a decision which has been abided by. Indeed, the extraordinary energy and volatility, the sadistic black comedy and sheer dramatic guts of Dickens' actual sentences are the *raisons d'être* of this piece. Returning to the original words – even for the singing in the show – was the main way in which I hoped to avoid any bowdlerisation of the tale. I wanted the show to be as alarming, as compelling and as wickedly comic as Dickens' words are. Of course, which words I have chosen to include, and which words I have chosen to omit, reveal what I personally care most about in this story. I hope.

The Question of Tone

'It is the custom on the stage, in all good murderous
melodrama, to present the tragic and the comic scenes,
in as regular alternation, as the layers of red and white in a
side of streaky bacon. The hero sinks upon his bed, weighed
down by misfortune; the next scene regales the audience with
comic song.'
Oliver Twist, Chapter 17

What do we mean by the word 'Dickensian'? Not, I think, simply subject matter taken from the lower depths of urban poverty. Rather, I think we mean a way of perceiving things, a distinctive way of dramatising what is seen.

The development of this adaptation was much informed by a reading of many of the earliest stage versions of the novel held in the Lord Chamberlain's Collection of the British Library. These nineteenth-century stagings – some made even before the final parts of the original, serialised novel had been published – have scripts of quite extraordinary ferocity and brevity. One of them gets the whole proceedings down to thirty handwritten pages, and still finds time for plenty of rambling low comedy from the Bumbles. They all seek to unashamedly achieve one objective, namely to rouse the audience. They want to provoke laughter, horror and ghoulish fascination; to stimulate sincere concern for the plight of orphaned children and sincere belief in the survival of innocence. To achieve this end, they employ the most remarkable combinations of comedy with horror, satire with sentiment. They demand that the audience enjoys the most alarming leaps of dramatic tone. They are also very fond of (and good at) employing those most powerful forms of theatrical shorthand, the baldly stated moral, the tableau and the melodrama. In doing all of this they are of course entirely in keeping with Dickens' own dramatic and dramatizing instincts in *Oliver Twist*.

Dickens is, paradoxically, the most serious of writers, in that he takes this task of engaging us, his audience, with such whole-hearted seriousness. I wanted to create an adaptation that would not shy away from this seriousness, but rather relish it; that would demand of its actors they engage with their audience above all else. This is why the script does not try to shift Dickens into some solid or polite middle ground of dialogue-based, psychologised 'literary' theatre, but lets his story move alarmingly (demandingly) through all its intensely felt and highly coloured original shifts of theatrical tone. It is only when melodrama is allowed to rub shoulders with psychodrama, when sensationalism combines with fierce and socially committed satire, that you arrive in the particular world of the dramatic imagination that we can only describe with the tautology 'Dickensian'.

Of course one of the particular challenges of tone, when putting *Oliver Twist* on stage, is that it is a story to which people want to bring their children. This, despite the fact that the story is horribly frightening, dealing as it does with the worst nightmares of childhood, and famously violent in its climactic scenes. This version is written on the assumption that violence on stage is best suggested, not literally recreated; and on the assumption that all the terrors Oliver endures are justified, if he endures them for a reason. If the company telling the story can communicate how much the makers of the story – author and actors alike – care, about the story and about Oliver, then his survival will seem earnt, not arbitrary. For the story to really work, neither the happy ending nor the darkness can be evaded, or fudged.

The Set

'Sudden shiftings of scene, and rapid changes of time and place, are not only sanctioned in books, by long usage, but are by many considered a great art.'
Oliver Twist, Chapter 17

The set and the script for the Lyric staging were developed simultaneously; the designer, lighting designer, producer, composer and director all contributed to the storyboard for the show. The movement of the story from scene to scene was visualised and drawn at the same time as it was written. The ideas of producing the show on a single setting, without any pauses for scene changes, and with all the mechanics of location-change being achieved by the company both in view of and in collusion with the audience, were there right from the start.

The first visual and physical inspiration for the set was a visit to the Chamber of Horrors at Madame Tussauds. This not only renewed my interest in the *unheimlich* appeal of waxworks, especially those depicting extreme violence, but also triggered in designer Rae Smith's imagination a connection between the sensationalist mechanics of Dickens' plot – its combination of creaky contrivance with uncanny power – with the mechanical toys which we now know as 'Penny Dreadful' machines. These are the sinister glass-fronted boxes which, in response to a child inserting the required coin, bring to life miniature tableaux of haunted houses, historic crimes or mildly erotic misdemeanours. One of these boxes, emptied and magnified, as if by a child's imagination, provided the basic setting. Of course, the early nineteenth century theatrical vocabulary of flyropes, trapdoors, footlights and two-dimensional scenery – so easily imagined at the Lyric, with its magnificent Victorian auditorium – also influenced both the design of the show and the script. All of these influences combined to allow, and indeed encourage, a script which cuts and dissolves from scene to scene without any establishing shots (to confuse matters by employing a cinematic vocabulary) – and, largely, without any narrative linking passages. Any future production of this script will of course have to find its own staging solutions, so I have kept any indications of how these transitions were achieved in the original production to a minimum. The only thing I would suggest is that the page-turning quality of *Oliver Twist* was one of the chief reasons for its initial success, and that any staging must be excited by that.

The Music

'The preliminaries adjusted, they proceeded with flourishes of most unmusical snatches of song, mingled with wild execrations.'
Oliver Twist, Chapter 26

The popular theatre which Dickens knew and loved was almost all, in the original sense of the word, melodrama; an evening at the theatre without live music barely existed in the first half of the nineteenth century. This script, too, is a melodrama, in that the telling of the story presupposes that the actors work with (and sometimes against) music in their telling of that story, and the creation of the different places and atmospheres which that story takes us to. The music in the Lyric's production was all adapted from popular early nineteenth-century music-hall numbers contemporary with the novel, and arranged for an authentically early Victorian combination of actors' voices, percussion, violin, serpent and hurdy-gurdy. Sometimes the company sang, as a chorus, directly across the footlights; sometimes members of the company played along with the singing; and sometimes members of the company played to give atmosphere or narrative urgency to otherwise wordless or purely physical sequences and moments in the show.

The script printed here does not indicate exactly when and where the music came; that would have cluttered it unnecessarily. Any future production must find its own solutions (possibly, in a different theatre, instrumental music could be dispensed with entirely) to the challenge of word-setting the collages of Dickens' prose that form the lyrics of the company choruses, and to the purely melodramatic sequences like Nancy's journey to London Bridge.

The Plot

'The good ended happily, and the bad unhappily. That is what fiction means.'
Miss Prism, *The Importance of Being Earnest*

The plot of *Oliver Twist* is a convoluted one at times; but its main shape has the force of a bad and deeply pleasurable dream. The version of the story I and my collaborators and actors have shaped here was driven by the simple desire to keep what we loved most, and were most moved by, and to cut the rest. Underneath the apparently picaresque characterisations, we felt, there is a story with a single over-riding desire; to find a family for its orphan hero. Every scene in the book can be read in this light; every character too. In the absence of Oliver's mother, Mr and Mrs Bumble, Mr and Mrs Sowerberry, even Noah Claypole and Charlotte all attempt, in their various twisted ways, to mother him. Fagin and Mr Brownlow, in their archetypically opposite worlds, construct surrogate families for Oliver. Everyone (even Mr Grimwig) is convinced that they know the right way for the boy to live. All of these conflicting dreams of family life, so deeply rooted in their creator's own childhood, are powerful; Nancy's dream of a possible home for Oliver – her determination that he will have the childhood she knows has been stolen from her – is so fierce, that it kills her.

In editing the plot, I also wanted to arrive at a script whose economy would encourage the actors to concentrate on trying to get back to the blunt realities of the original cast-list. Nancy is a teenage prostitute with a violent owner, not a musical-comedy star; the boys Fagin says he finds sleeping rough at Kings Cross are very like the teenagers who still sleep rough there; Bill is a violent housebreaker, and a coward; Fagin is Jewish, and his vicious rage is that of someone who lives excluded from everything we might conceiveably call society.

Some of the events of the great final working-out of the story may surprise audiences who only know it from films. I've kept what for me is the greatest and strangest scene of the book, where, on the night before his death, Fagin goes mad with terror, and in his madness realises that Oliver is 'somehow the cause of all this'. I've taken Mr Brownlow and Rose seriously. I've dared to kill off not just Nancy and Bill, but Fagin and the Dodger, as Dickens does. I've even dared to believe, as Dickens did, that after all the strange, violent parodies of family life that claim him – the brutal workhouse of the Bumbles, the gothic funeral-parlour of the Sowerberries, the nightmare inversion of all maternal values in Fagin's den – the motherless Oliver's destiny is the one we must all, despite our evidence to the contrary, believe in: safety.

Neil Bartlett
Lyric Hammersmith
February 2004

This version of *Oliver Twist* was first performed at the Lyric Hammersmith on 25 February 2004, in a production created by the following company:

Nicholas Asbury: Mrs Sowerberry (a sour, vixenish woman); Bill Sikes (a brutal thief and housebreaker); Workhouse Inmate No. Seven; A Policeman; A Member of the Workhouse Board; A Workhouse Boy

Ryan Early: Charley Bates (a thief, one of Fagin's apprentices); A Doctor; A Member of the Workhouse Board; A Mourner; A Smartly Dressed Servant

Michael Feast: Fagin, a receiver of stolen goods

Nicholas Goode: Toby Crackit (a housebreaker); Workhouse Inmate No. Five; A Member of the Workhouse Board; A Mourner; The Last Minute Witness; The Second Policeman

Gregor Henderson-Begg: Noah Claypole (a charity boy, apprenticed to Mr Sowerberry); Tom Chitling (one of Fagin's apprentices); Workhouse Inmate No. Four; A Workhouse Boy; A Member of the Workhouse Board

Paul Hunter: Mr Bumble (a Parish Beadle); Bystander No. Three

Derek Hutchinson: Mr Sowerberry (a parochial undertaker); Mr Fang (an overbearing police-magistrate); Mr Grimwig (a friend of Mr Brownlow's); a Boy in Fagin's Gang; Workhouse Inmate No. Two; A Member of the Workhouse Board; Bystander No. Four; Workhouse Boy

Jordan Metcalfe: Oliver Twist, a poor, nameless orphan boy

Owen Sharpe: John Dawkins, 'The Artful Dodger' (a young pickpocket in the service of Fagin)

Kellie Shirley: Nancy (a thief in Fagin's service); The corpse of Oliver's Mother; A Mourner; Bystander No. Five; A Workhouse Boy; A Member of the Board

Thomas Wheatley: Mr Brownlow (a benevolent old gentleman); Workhouse Inmate No. Six; A Workhouse Boy; A Mourner; The Chairman of the Workhouse Board

Louise Yates: Rose Brownlow (daughter of the preceding); Workhouse Inmate No. One; Charlotte (servant to Mrs Sowerberry); A Boy in Fagin's Gang; A Member of the Workhouse Board; A Workhouse Boy; Bystander No. One

Brigid Zengeni: Mrs Corney (Matron of a Workhouse, after married to Mr Bumble); Bystander No. Two

CREATIVE TEAM

Adapted and directed by Neil Bartlett

Designed by Rae Smith
Lighting by Paule Constable
Music by Gerard McBurney
Musical Direction by Simon Deacon
Movement by Struan Leslie
Sound by Nick Manning

Company Stage Manager: Claire Bryan
Technical Stage Manager on Tour: Darren Joyce
Deputy Stage Manager: Heidi Lennard
Assistant Stage Manager: Sarah Hunter
Wardrobe Assistant: Katie Moore

Costumes made by Lyric Hammersmith Wardrobe
Set and props made by Scott Fleary Ltd

Casting: Siobhan Bracke
Production Photography: John Haynes
Press Representative: Bridget Thornborrow   020 7247 7737
Tour Marketing: Mark Slaughter
Tour Workshop Leader: Michael Burgess

The Oliver Twist Education pack has been produced with the generous support of The Ernest Cook Trust.

With thanks to the following actors and artists who contributed to the workshops in which the first ideas for Oliver Twist were developed: Adjoa Andoh, Bette Bourne, Hayley Carmichael, Patti Clare, Guy Dartnell, Glen Hill, Beverley Klein, Charmian Hoare, Bijan Sheibani, Mhairi Steenbock,Tim Sutton and Miltos Yerolemou. These workshops were supported by the Calouste Gulbenkian Foundation.

The music of the Lyric production was adapted by Gerard McBurney from music-hall and parlour songs by W. Wilson (*The Lost Child*, 1834), John Hobbes (*Eulalie*, 1844) and George Robey/C.W. Murphy (*A Thing He Had Never Done Before*), and a scene from the ballad-opera*The Castle of Andalusia* by William Shield, 1820.

ACT ONE

Scene One

Treats of the place where Oliver Twist was born, and of the circumstances attending his birth

Silence.

A single figure (the actor who will play the DODGER, though his costume does not yet declare as much) is there on the stage, intently reading a book. Really intently.

Another figure comes on and reads over his shoulder, and another and another, until there are eleven of them – the COMPANY.

They look at the audience. They have a story to tell. They have a challenge:

DODGER: It is a solemn thing to hear, in a darkened room, the voice of a child…recounting a catalogue of the evils and calamities which hard men have brought upon him. Oh!, if we bestowed but one thought on that dark evidence of human error; if we heard for but one instant, in imagination, that deep testimony, which no power can stifle and no pride shut out – where would be injury, and injustice, and cruelty, and wrong…? …Two, three, four:

Unexpectedly,

Ensemble sung chorus

a capella, harmonised:

COMPANY: **There are some people, of so refined and delicate a nature,**
They would safely relegate to other centuries all images of vice, of hunger and of horror;

Such may object, it being written in 1837, our tale is
now not so much true as old;
Well we are glad to have its moral doubted, for in that
we find assurance that it needed to be told:
To be sure, it is a work of fiction;
An impossibility, an anomaly, an apparent
contradiction;
For it finds Hope, flourishing, where all hope was
past;
It shows, in little Oliver, the principle of Good
surviving through every adverse circumstance, and
triumphing at the last!!

The Story Begins

DODGER: On...a day and date which we need not take upon
ourselves to repeat, since it can be of no possible
consequence – there was born...the item of mortality
whose name is prefixed to tonight's story.

He was born in a workhouse –

*As the DODGER turns the page, suddenly, very swiftly, rather
alarmingly and without any command apparently being given,
the arrange themselves into a*

TABLEAU

FEATURING OLIVER'S DYING MOTHER, A NEWBORN BABY, A
DOCTOR, MRS CORNEY AND SEVERAL ELDERLY FEMALE
WORKHOUSE INMATES.

*The image and the voices of the people in it are expressive of
regimentedness, callousness, misery, poverty and negligence.*

For some time after he was ushered into this world –

INMATE ONE: This world of sorrow and trouble...

DODGER: It remained a matter of considerable doubt whether
the child would survive to bear any name at all...

INMATE TWO: In which case, this memoir need never have appeared –

DODGER: Or if it had, would possess the inestimable merit of being the most concise and faithful specimen of dramatic biography extant.

However…

After a few seconds…

After a few struggles…

The child breathed.

The sound of a baby choking into life and starting to cry as it is passed carelessly from INMATE to INMATE.

If he'd known he was an orphan, perhaps he would have cried even louder.

DOCTOR: It's all over Mrs Thingummy.

MRS CORNEY: Ah, poor dear so it is. Poor dear.

DOCTOR: A good looking girl, too.

MRS CORNEY: Found lying in the street.

DODGER: Where she came from, or where she was going to, nobody knew.

DOCTOR: The old story. No wedding ring, I see.

INMATES: Ah!

DOCTOR: It's very likely the child will be troublesome. Give it gruel, if it is.

MRS CORNEY: Yes Doctor.

The INMATES are busy with the baby; MRS CORNEY is left alone with the body. She sees something around its neck, and steals it.

Suddenly, a terrible noise; workhouse bell or alarm or rattle.

Scene Two

Oliver Twist's growth, education and board

Enter MR BUMBLE. The action of transforming from INMATES back into COMPANY indicates the workhouse routine, the preparations for daily feeding time of the workhouse boys; a table, bowls, gruel et cetera.

A sign has been put up, reading 10.

MR BUMBLE reads this to the audience as if giving a lesson to stupid illiterate children who he beats when they get it wrong.

MR BUMBLE: Ten – one, two, three, four, five, six, seven, eight, nine…ten!!! Ten years old already. Not that he knows he is.

MRS CORNEY: (*Busy with the preparations.*) The boy's a fool.

MR BUMBLE: And sickly, Mrs Corney, obstinately sickly.

MRS CORNEY: Well Mr Bumble hard as it is for us has charge of them to see the little ones suffer before our very eyes, they will sicken…they get themselves smothered, they fall into the fire, they get themselves scalded to death when there's a washing… Still, I always say, they may have no father and no mother but they're neat, they're clean, they says prayers every night for the people who feeds them, and sevenpence halfpenny per head per week is a good round diet for any child…

MR BUMBLE: And notwithstanding the most superlative, and, I may say, supernat'ral exertions on the part of this parish Mrs Corney, we have never been able to discover his mother's settlement, name, or condition.

MRS CORNEY: How comes he to have any name at all, then.

MR BUMBLE: I inwented it.

MRS CORNEY: You, Mr Bumble? What a literary character you are.

MR BUMBLE: I, Mrs Corney. I name my fondlings in alphabetical order. The last was a Swubble, the next as came was a Unwin, the next Vilkins, but this was a T. Twist, Mrs Bumble. Oliver Twist.

MRS CORNEY: Hmph!

OLIVER is discovered or revealed.

MR BUMBLE: Oliver Twist. A naughty orphan, which nobody can't love.

MR BUMBLE raps on the floor with his staff.

TABLEAU

THE BOYS SAY GRACE.

BOYS: Our Father

Which art in heaven –

MRS CORNEY: We humbly entreat you to be made good, virtuous, and obedient, and to be guarded from all the sins and vices of appetite. Amen.

BOYS: (*Sing.*) **Amen.**

A second rap on the floor from MR BUMBLE; it is feeding time. A desperate scraping of bowls with spoon, followed by silence. In this silence, a crescendo

TABLEAU

OF THE BOYS 'DESPERATE WITH HUNGER AND RECKLESS WITH MISERY'.

The boys elect OLIVER as their representative.

OLIVER: Please.

Please, Sir, I want some more.

Mr BUMBLE gazes at him in stupefied astonishment; MRS CORNEY is paralysed with wonder; the BOYS with fear.

MR BUMBLE: What?

OLIVER: Please, sir, I want some more.

MRS CORNEY screams in horror. There is a general start. Horror is depicted on every countenance. Manic rearrangement into a new

TABLEAU

OF THE WORKHOUSE BOARD.

MR BUMBLE: I beg your pardon gentlemen. Oliver Twist has asked for more!

THE CHAIRMAN OF THE BOARD: For *more*!!

BOARDMEMBER: He does know he's an orphan, I suppose?

MR BUMBLE: He does.

BOARDMEMBER: Knows he's got no father or mother?

THE CHAIRMAN OF THE BOARD: That boy will be hung.

BOARD: Hear hear!!

THE CHAIRMAN OF THE BOARD: I know that boy will be hung.

BOARD: Hung!

The BOARD, removing their wigs, sing the next a capella chorus.

COMPANY: **Whether the life of Oliver Twist has this violent termination or no...**
It is our purpose, tonight – eventually – to show.

THE CHAIRMAN OF THE BOARD: Mr Bumble!

The BOARD go back into character.

MR BUMBLE: Sir!

MR BUMBLE's cane has come out and is swishing in anticipation…

THE CHAIRMAN OF THE BOARD: Post the bill!!

MR BUMBLE: I will Sir!!

The BOARD chunter off, as a bill in Roman capitals of a gigantic size is pasted up outside the workhouse gate, announcing

BY ORDER OF THIS PARISH, FOR SALE, A PAROCHIAL PRENTICE-BOY
FIVE POUNDS
TO ANYBODY WHO WILL TAKE
OLIVER TWIST OFF THE HANDS OF THIS PARISH

MR BUMBLE: (*Reading again.*) Five pounds; Oliver Twist; anybody.

Oliver!

OLIVER: Sir.

MR BUMBLE: Oliver, the kind and blessed gentlemen which is so many parents to you, Oliver, you having not one of your own, being a naughty orphan which nobody can't love (*Swishing of the cane.*) are a going to prentice you and set you up in life, and make a man of you. (*Swish.*)

(*Exhibiting the child to the audience, and attempting to raise a bid from the audience.*) Five Pounds. Five pounds a Porochial Prentiss. Anybody…

Come now gentlemen – a critical moment of the boys fate gentlemen – bow to the gentlemen Oliver – Oliver… Don't cry. That's a very foolish action sir. Look happy. Happy! Well! Well! – Of all the ungratefullest –

MR BUMBLE is drowned out by –

Scene Three

Oliver prentissed

The sound of music; THE FUNERAL MARCH.

A funeral procession enters, as if Death had come for the child.

This procession is lead by MR and MRS SOWERBERRY, with NOAH and CHARLOTTE. Black drapery, hatbands and plumes, mutes and band of MOURNERS providing the music.

MR BUMBLE: Mr Sowerberry sir, you don't know anybody who wants a boy, do you? – a porochial prentis? (*Indicating the bill.*) Liberal terms, Mr Sowerberry, liberal terms. Five. Pounds.

MR SOWERBERRY: I should say three pounds ten was plenty.

MRS SOWERBERRY: I should say it was ten shillings too much –

MR BUMBLE: Four pounds –

MRS SOWERBERRY: Three pounds –

MR BUMBLE: Three pounds fifteen –

MRS SOWERBERRY: Three pounds –

MR BUMBLE: Sold. He's just the boy for you, ma'am. He wants the stick, now and then, but it does him good. Oliver!

OLIVER: Yes sir.

MR BUMBLE: Hold your head up. (*He doesn't.*) Well! Of all the ungratefullest, and worst-disposed boys as I ever seed, you is the worst, Oliver. (*The cane rises…*)

OLIVER: No – no Sir. But I am…I am so…

MR BUMBLE: So what?

OLIVER: Lonely, sir.

MR BUMBLE: (*Disengaging himself with difficulty, coughs, hemms.*) Well then, you…you be a good boy. Good.

OLIVER: Yes Sir.

Exit MR BUMBLE, moved despite himself, shooing off the mourners.

MRS SOWERBERRY: He's very small.

MR SOWERBERRY: He'll grow, my dear, he'll grow.

MRS SOWERBERRY: I dare say he will, on our victuals and our drink.

Charlotte! Give this boy some of the cold bits that were put by for Trip. I dare say the boy isn't too dainty to eat 'em – are you, boy.

OLIVER: No mam.

They watch in silent horror as they witness the terrible avidity with which OLIVER, eating on the floor like a dog, tears the bits asunder.

CHARLOTTE: How 'orrible.

MR SOWERBERRY: Horrible.

CHARLOTTE: Dreadful.

MRS SOWERBERRY: Dreadful. Well, have you done.

OLIVER: Yes.

MRS SOWERBERRY: Well get down stairs, little bag of bones. You don't mind sleeping under the counter, I suppose, not that it doesn't much matter whether you do or don't, you can't sleep anywhere else. Come on, don't keep me here all night.

OLIVER is put to bed. Scrutinised by the SOWERBERRIES, he goes to sleep.

MR SOWERBERRY: My dear.

MRS SOWERBERRY: Yes.

MR SOWERBERRY: Nothing my dear, nothing. I was only going to say…a very-good-looking boy, this, my dear.

MRS SOWERBERRY: He needs be, he eats enough.

MR SOWERBERRY: Such an expression of melancholy in his face… In a black suit, and hatband, he would surely excite great emotion at funerals, my dear, great emotion. In the mothers.

MRS SOWERBERRY: Very novel I'm sure.

MR SOWERBERRY: Do boys dream, do you think, my dear.

MRS SOWERBERRY: Don't ask me. I don't want to intrude on anybody's secrets. What's he got to be dreaming of? (*Exiting.*)

MR SOWERBERRY: That he is in a coffin, perhaps; and being laid down to sleep for ever.

TABLEAU

OLIVER ASLEEP AMONGST THE COFFINS.

With MR SOWERBERRY like Death standing over him.

Jump cut; next morning.

Banging on a door.

NOAH: Open the door, will yer.

OLIVER unlocks the door and lets NOAH in.

Yer the new boy, aint yer.

OLIVER: Yes sir.

NOAH: How old are yer?

OLIVER: Ten.

NOAH: Yer don't know who I am, do yer.

OLIVER: No sir.

NOAH: I'm Mister Noah Claypole, and you're under me.
Which means I can whop yer, whenever I wants ter.

*Enter CHARLOTTE with a breakfast tray for NOAH; she
lovingly feeds him bacon, as –*

CHARLOTTE: Oliver, shut that door at Mister Noah's back,
take your tea away and drink it over there – (*As he does.*)
and make haste; they'll be wanting you to mind the shop.

NOAH: (*Eating bacon.*) Workhus…

CHARLOTTE: Lor, Noah, let the boy alone!

NOAH: How is yer Mother, workhus.

OLIVER: She's dead.

CHARLOTTE: Oh!

NOAH: What she die of, workhus? – a broken heart!! –(*Sings.
'Tol lol de rol' et cetera to the tune of* THE FUNERAL MARCH,
*while acting out dying of a broken heart, trying to make
OLIVER cry – CHARLOTTE joins the game.*) Oh! – aaaah –
is you a snivelling, Oliver?

OLIVER: No.

NOAH: Oh?

OLIVER: No.

NOAH: Cause yer know, workhus, it can't be helped now, and
I'm very sorry for it – and I'm sure we all are – and pity

yer very much, but yer must know, Workhus, yer Mother was a regular right-down bad-un.

CHARLOTTE: Oh!

NOAH: A regular right-down bad'un, Workhus, and it's a great deal better that she died when she did, or else she'd have been hard labouring by now, or transported, or which is more likely than either…hung!!!

OLIVER, being goaded by the Taunts of Noah, rouses into Action, and rather astonishes everyone; i.e. he wallops NOAH. CHARLOTTE and NOAH then proceed to beat him up, during which –

Charlotte!

CHARLOTTE: O you little wretch!

NOAH: Help!

CHARLOTTE: You little un-grate- ful, mur-der-rous, horrid villain!

NOAH: Help! The new boy's a murdering of me! Oliver's gone mad! Help! Charlotte! Missis!

Enter MRS SOWERBERRY.

MRS SOWERBERRY: Aaaaaargh!

MRS SOWERBERRY holds OLIVER so that CHARLOTTE can punch him while she slaps him; once he is thus secured NOAH gets up and hits him from behind. They lock OLIVER up in a big box or a coffin. OLIVER continues to kick and scream inside it.

This being done, MRS SOWERBERRY sinks into a chair.

Oh! –

CHARLOTTE: Bless her, she's going off. A glass of water, Noah –

Exit NOAH.

MRS SOWERBERRY: Oh! Charlotte!

CHARLOTTE: Ma'am, that boy's a dreadful creature; send for the police officers!

NOAH: (*Returning.*) Send for the millingtary!

MRS SOWERBERRY: And no man in the house –

NOAH throws his glass of water in her face as enter MR SOWERBERRY –

– Oh!!!!

NOAH: Oh!!!

CHARLOTTE: Oh, sir – Oliver, sir, Oliver!

MR SOWERBERRY: Not run away; he hasn't run away!!

CHARLOTTE: Not run away sir; he's turned wicious.

NOAH: He tried to murder me, sir, and then he tried to murder Charlotte, and then Missis. Oh, what dreadful pain it is, please, sir, oh, the agony, the agony sir, the pain et cetera.

Suddenly enter:

MR BUMBLE: Murder! I knew it! I felt a strange presentiment from the very first that that owdacious young savage would come to be hung.

MRS CORNEY: Bad blood Mr Bumble. That mother of his made her way here against difficulties and pain that would have killed any well-disposed woman, weeks before.

MR BUMBLE kicks or thumps the box in which OLIVER is locked.

MR BUMBLE: Oliver –

OLIVER: Let me out!!!

MR BUMBLE: – do you know this here voice, Oliver?

OLIVER: Yes!!

MR BUMBLE: Aint you afraid of it Sir? Aint you a – trembling?

OLIVER: No!!

ALL: Oh!!!!!!

MRS CORNEY: Mr Bumble, he must be mad –

MR BUMBLE: It's not Madness maam. It's Meat.

MRS SOWERBERRY: Meat?

MR BUMBLE: Meat. You've over-fed him maam. If you had kept the boy on gruel, this would never have happened.

MRS SOWERBERRY: Dear, dear! – this is what comes of being liberal.

MR SOWERBERRY loses his patience and thwacks the box.

MR SOWERBERRY: Oliver, you're a nice boy, aint you!

OLIVER: He called my mother names!

MR SOWERBERRY: Well she deserved it!

OLIVER: She didn't!!

ALL: OH YES SHE DID!! –

MRS SOWERBERRY: (*Punctuating her remarks with a vicious thrashing of the box – she would clearly like to be thrashing the child in it.*) – you ill-conditioned! naughty! hardened! bad-disposed boy! born of a bad mother! born to go wrong at one time or another! born to the misery of an idle life! lazy! ungrateful!…ungrateful!…oh!

A few more gratuitous thwacks, kicks and thrashes on the box, and they all exit. Silence.

Scene Four

Oliver walks to London. He encounters on the road a strange sort of young gentleman.

When they've all gone DODGER comes back on. With the book.

DODGER: It was not until he was left alone that Oliver gave way to his feelings. Hiding his face in his hands, he wept – wept such tears as, God send for the credit of our natures, few so young may ever have cause to pour out before him.

And then, with noone there to see him or to hear him… Oliver decided…

He had better try to live.

DODGER opens the box, and OLIVER looks out of it, during:

It was a cold, dark night. The stars seemed, to a boy's eyes, farther from the earth than they had ever been before.There was no wind.

DODGER is not so much narrating as egging him on.

The first rays of light struggled though the shutters.

OLIVER listens and looks carefully around.

He got up, and he unbarred the door.

OLIVER gets out of the box.

One last look around – one moment's pause of hesitation – and he was in the open street.

DODGER closes and clears the box. Now the sun begins to slowly rise on an open landscape.

By eight o'clock he was nearly five miles away from the town.

MR BUMBLE and MR SOWERBERRY cross as if in pursuit; OLIVER hides behind DODGER.

MR SOWERBERRY: You won't spare him Mr Bumble –

MR BUMBLE: No, I will not, sir. I never do anything with a
boy, without stripes and bruises.

They exit.

DODGER: He hid behind hedges.

Another four miles and he gained the high-road. At noon,
he sat down for a rest by the side of a milestone.

(*He reads the stone to OLIVER.*) Seventy miles to London.

London.

London!!

Nobody could ever find him there! No lad of spirit need
want in London; there are ways of living in that vast city
which those who have been bred up in country parts have
no idea of. It is the very place for a homeless boy…who
feels cold, and hungry, and has no-one to care for and no-
one to take care of him…a naughty boy, which nobody
can't love…a boy that everybody hates.

The sun is now blazing.

The first day, Oliver walked twenty miles. Then, being
very tired, he slept. Then got up. And walked. Then slept.
Then got up. And walked. For seven days.

On the seventh morning, he got to a place called Barnet;
his feet were bleeding, and he was too tired even to beg.

People stared at him, but noone troubled themselves to
inquire how the boy came to be there. Sat upon a cold
door-step. Well you don't, do you?

And then – (*DODGER starts to transform himself into THE
DODGER.*) – he observed that another boy – a dirty,
common-faced, strange boy – was surveying him. Most
earnestly.

The DODGER pockets the book, indicating that he's perfectly capable of busking it from now on.

DODGER: Hello my covey. What's the row.

OLIVER: I am very hungry and tired. I have walked a long way.

DODGER Oh, I see. Going to London?

OLIVER: Yes.

DODGER: Got any lodgings?

OLIVER: No.

DODGER: Money?

OLIVER: No.

DODGER: (*Whistles.*) And I suppose you want some place to sleep in tonight, don't you?

OLIVER: Yes.

DODGER: Well…don't you fret your eyelids on that score. I know a 'spectable old genelman as lives in London, what'll give you lodgings for nothink, and never ask for the change – that is, if it's a genelman he knows interduces you. And does he know me? Oh no. Not in the least. By no means. Certainly not. John – also known as Jack – Dawkins, Mister; and, to his hintimates, the Dodger, Artful.

OLIVER: Twist. Oliver.

DODGER: Twist Oliver; on your pins. There! Now…Morrice! Right…here goes…

THE DODGER'S FIRST PATTER NUMBER – a bit like a cabbie doing The Knowledge of the route from Barnet to Field Lane, which is where FAGIN's den is.

Barnet…Whetstone, Finchley, Archway, Holloway;

(*Sings tune of* Pop Goes The Weasel.) **All the way down Upper Street, down to the Angel,** cross the Angel; St John's Road; left – shortcut, Arlington Street, back of Sadlers Wells –

right; Exmouth St; Exmouth Street Market; left; down the passage by the side of the old workhouse (*Spits.*) cross Hatton Wall; down Little Saffron Hill; cross Charles Street – gets a bit narrow, gets a bit muddy, a bit…impregnated – down Great Saffron Hill, down to the bottom…of the hill. Field Lane –

just off Faringdon Road, round the back of Faringdon tube…

Shops – all boarded up; dogs, children – at this time of night!; public houses – wrangling, screaming, wallowing, all a bit drunken, all a bit dirty; beer, fried fish: a bit… wretched; dark; broken, greasy, a bit…filthy –

OLIVER makes a move to run away – DODGER grabs him by the collar.

– ah, ah, ah…through a door; down a passage; close the door…

Scene Five

Oliver meets a pleasant old gentleman

The DODGER whistles.

CHARLEY: (*A voice behind a door.*) Now then!

DODGER: Plummy and Slam!

Six of FAGIN's boys emerge from the woodwork, all in strange lurid clothes, as the footlights begin to glow. Humming and whistling…

CHARLEY: There's two of you. Who's the other one?

DODGER: A new pal.

TOM: Where did he come from?

DODGER: Greenland. Where's Fagin?

TOBY: In the back, sortin the wipes.

OLIVER is surrounded by and trapped amidst these alarming creatures, who are smoking and drinking. They look as though they might do something dreadful to him – but then –there, suddenly, in the midst of them, as if he had come from nowhere, is FAGIN.

The DODGER whispers something to him. FAGIN turns round, and grins at OLIVER.

TABLEAU

THE MERRY OLD GENTLEMAN AND HIS BOYS

Then:

DODGER: This is him, Fagin; my friend, Oliver Twist.

FAGIN bows and takes his hand.

FAGIN: I do hope I shall have the honour of your intimate acquaintance, my dear.

Boys…

The boys move in to be introduced…

Mr Toby Crackit… Mr Charley Bates…

TOM: Mr Tom Chitlin –

The boys begin to rifle OLIVER's pockets, steal his cap et cetera, and FAGIN beats them off with his toasting fork.

FAGIN: We are very glad to see you, Oliver, very. Charley, take off the sausages…

CHARLEY: Yes Fagin.

FAGIN: Thank you Charley. Suppertime, Oliver. Dodger, draw a tub near the fire for Oliver.

The BOYS prepare to eat; an echo of the mealtime preparations in the Workshouse.

Under FAGIN's fierce parental eye, each boy in turn is served a sausage, and wolfs it.

Are you hungry, Oliver?

OLIVER: Yes Sir.

He is served with his sausage, and wolfs it…

FAGIN: Well eat your share, and then I'll mix you a nice glass of hot gin and water.

It is immediately provided.

Drink it off directly, there's another gentleman wanting the tumbler.

Would you like some more, Oliver?

But having drunk the gin, OLIVER immediately falls asleep.

Put him to bed, Dodger.

And the rest of you. Bed!

Swiftly, blankets et cetera…

Now go to sleep.

Go to sleep.

FAGIN dims the lights, and looks round at his little sleeping team, huddled in corners with their sleeping bags…

– Good dogs. Clever dogs… And you Dodger!

He checks on OLIVER, who is already asleep. He locks the door. He looks at OLIVER again.

Face like an angel.

FAGIN looks at the audience…

Now that he is sure they are all asleep, he locks the door, then he opens a trap in the floor and takes out a small box. It is full of his treasures.

…Good dogs…staunch to the last. Never tell the old parson where the loot is, would you?

(*To the audience.*) And why would they, eh? It wouldn't loosen the knot, wouldn't keep the drop up a moment longer. No, no, no! What a fine thing capital punishment is…dead men never repent…dead boys neither; never talk, never bring any awkward stories to light…

Beautiful…beau-ti-ful things.

He fingers his treasures…

Suddenly FAGIN realises that OLIVER is awake and spying on him. He pulls a knife.

FAGIN: Why are you awake?

OLIVER: I couldn't sleep.

FAGIN: What did you see?

OLIVER: Nothing –

FAGIN: Are you sure?

OLIVER: Yes.

FAGIN: Of course you are. Tush tush. I only tried to frighten you. You're a brave boy. Ha! ha! you're a brave boy, Oliver! Did you see any of those pretty things, just then?

OLIVER: Yes, sir.

FAGIN: Ah! They – they're mine, Oliver. My little property. All I have to live on in my old age. It's a poor trade, you

see, and everybody has to be careful for himself, Oliver!…
Some conjurors say that number three is the magic
number, and some say number seven, but it's neither,
Oliver, neither. It's number one.

OLIVER: Number one?

FAGIN: And in a little community like ours, my dear, we
have a general number one; that is, you can't consider
yourself as number one, without considering me as the
same. You see we are all so mixed up together, and
identified in our interests. Remember that, Oliver. Now go
back to sleep… Good boy. Good boy. Sweet dreams.

OLIVER is asleep.

Sweet dreams.

*FAGIN looks at the boy; then looks at the audience watching
him do it; then blows out the candle, as we cross-cut to a
hallucination, a dream, during which OLIVER tosses and
turns in his sleep.*

Scene Six

Which is short, but a key to one that will follow
when its time arrives

*MR BUMBLE and MRS CORNEY walk in through one of the
walls and cross the scene like sharks drifting through a tank.*

MR BUMBLE: Stole it, my fascinator?

MRS CORNEY: When she was stone dead I stole it – and
yes, it is gold, I tell you. Gold that might have saved her
life, had she not hid it. That child, Mr Bumble, that child
was the offspring of a guilty union.

MR BUMBLE: Yes, my love.

FAGIN closes the door behind them as they leave. If there was music during the above, it cuts.

Scene Seven

Oliver becomes better acquainted with the merry old gentleman and his hopeful pupils

FAGIN: Oliver. Oliver, wake up.

OLIVER wakes up with a start from his nightmare of being back in the workshouse.

Ssh ssh ssh; I wouldn't be so cruel as to send you back, would I?

OLIVER wonders how FAGIN guessed what he was dreaming about.

It's breakfast time. Are you hungry, Oliver?

OLIVER: Yes sir.

FAGIN whistles and we jump cut to a cold bright morning. At top speed the boys pack their bedding away and produce hot rolls and ham from their hats; hot coffee appears; this is all done like a conjuring trick. The family has its breakfast together as –

FAGIN: Well boys I hope you've been at work when out this morning.

DODGER: Hard –

CHARLEY: – As nails.

FAGIN: Good boys, good boys. And what have you got, Dodger.

DODGER – again like a magician – dazzling OLIVER – produces a watch and snuff box and spectacles…

37

DODGER: …and…a couple of wallets.

FAGIN: Lined?

DODGER: Pretty well.

FAGIN: Not so heavy as they might be, but very neat and nicely made. Ingenious workman, ain't he, Oliver, eh?

OLIVER: Very.

CHARLEY: Ha! Ha! Ha!

FAGIN: And what have you got Charley.

CHARLEY: Wipes.

FAGIN: And very good ones, very – you'd like to be able to make pockethandkerchiefs as easy as Charley Bates, wouldn't you, Oliver.

OLIVER: Very much if you'll teach me.

CHARLEY: Ain't he green, Fagin!!

CHARLEY laughs his laugh again and FAGIN shuts him up.

DODGER: He'll know better, bye-and-bye, won't yer, Oliver?

FAGIN: Shall we play our game, boys.

FAGIN loads up his pockets with all the morning's loot and pretends to be an old gentleman walking up and down the street looking in shop windows, humming a little tune and constantly checking that there no thieves about and checking his pockets. He invites TOM to have a go at picking his pockets. Every times he feels a hand in his pocket, he cries out. TOM fails once too often, and FAGIN chastises him.

FAGIN: No! No! You ill-conditioned, naughty, miserable! idle! lazy! ungrateful!

As FAGIN continues MRS SOWERBERRY's imprecations against bad children, NANCY enters.

NANCY: Ill-treating the boys again I see Fagin.

FAGIN: Nancy, good morning.

NANCY: And what's this.

FAGIN: The new boy. Oliver, Miss Nancy.

NANCY: How old are you?

OLIVER: Ten.

NANCY: God help you.

FAGIN: We were just showing Oliver our game Nancy. Charley, Dodger – Nancy…

NANCY: Put me up a drain – without poison in it – and I might.

FAGIN indicates someone to pour NANCY a gin as requested. The game continues, with NANCY, after she's had her drink, joining in, and CHARLEY and DODGER proving themselves expert, taking from FAGIN, with extraordinary rapidity, snuff-box, note-case, watch and chain and handkerchief. Applause; which we see OLIVER join in. This is noted by FAGIN.

FAGIN: (*To the audience.*) Good boys. See what a pride they take in their profession! See what a pride they take in their profession, Oliver. Beautiful, ain't it? Right; pad the hoof the lot of you. (*As the boys exit.*)

NANCY: Bill says where's the blunt.

FAGIN: My dear, I haven't so much as would –

NANCY: He don't want to know how much you've got, he just needs it this morning.

FAGIN: (*Handing over money.*) Tell Bill, I know he'll do me a good turn another time, eh?

NANCY: That's all, is it?

FAGIN: All. Good morning Nancy.

She goes, and FAGIN locks the door behind her.

There now, what a pleasant life, isn't it. Make 'em your models, my dear, make 'em your models, do everything they bid you, and take their advice in all matters; – 'specially the Dodger's – he'll be a great man, that boy, and could make you one too.

Is my handkerchief hanging out of my pocket, Oliver?

OLIVER: Yes sir.

FAGIN: See if you can take it out, without my feeling it, as you saw the other boys do when we played our game… Is it gone?

OLIVER: Here it is sir.

FAGIN: No! You are a clever boy. I never saw a sharper lad. Here's a shilling for you. Now remember; if you go on, in this way, you'll be a great man – the greatest man of the time.

FAGIN goes to leave him alone and locked up.

OLIVER: I should like to go out sir. With the others.

FAGIN: Should you Oliver should you.

OLIVER: Yes sir.

FAGIN: Already.

OLIVER: Yes sir.

FAGIN: …well.

He whistles.

CHARLEY and DODGER, using a streetname sign, take us to a street in Clerkenwell.

Scene Eight

Oliver becomes better acquainted with the characters of his new associates, and purchases experience at a high price

As if the game of learning how to be a pickpocket were continuing, FAGIN brings on MR BROWNLOW. DODGER hands MR BROWNLOW the book, in which he buries his nose. FAGIN, once everything is set up to his satisfaction, leaves them to it.

CHARLEY and DODGER show OLIVER how to pretend to be sauntering along: TOM and TOBY keep cavy.

DODGER suddenly stops and lays his finger on his lips.

OLIVER: What's the matter?

DODGER: Sssh! The old cove with the book. Standing by the bookstall. See him?

OLIVER: Yes.

DODGER: He'll do.

CHARLEY: Prime.

DODGER: 'Ere, Twist; watch this.

> *OLIVER watches with horror and alarm, looking on with his eyelids as wide open as they will possible go, as DODGER and CHARLEY give a running commentary on the execution of the theft.*

> One very respectable old personage, wearing…velvet, nice…and –

CHARLEY: Gold spectacles.

DODGER: Reading away, as hard as if he was at home in his very own chair. Which he very possibly fancies he is; can't see anything but his book –

CHARLEY: – can't see the street, can't see any boys –

DODGER: – can't see Charley, can't see me…plunging the hand

Into the pocket…

And drawing from thence…

The wipe;

Handing the same to my assistant Mr Charley Bates – I thank you –

And then…

Scarpering round the corner!!

OLIVER is rooted to the spot.

MR BROWNLOW puts his hand to his pocket, misses his handkerchief, turns sharply round. He sees the boy.

MR BROWNLOW: Stop – Thief!!

With OLIVER still frozen to the spot, a CROWD OF BYSTANDERS emerge to deliver the following joyously violent chorus:

BYSTANDERS: Stop Thief!
Soon as they heard it, they –
Stop Thief!
Up go the windows, and –
Stop Thief!
Out run the people, and –
Stop Thief!
The butcher the baker and
Stop Thief!

The milkman the schoolboys and –
Stop Thief!
Stop Thief!
Stop Thief!

The chorus lifts to full song.

There is a passion for hunting something deeply implanted in the human breast;

Even when that something is but one wretched breathless boy;

As he pants with exhaustion, they chase him without rest;

And as his strength decreases, and the crowd gains upon him, they whoop and scream with joy.

OLIVER is knocked down.

TABLEAU

Of Bystanders Gathered Round And Jostling For A Glimpse Of The Fallen Child.

Then, in Punch and Judy voices:

BYSTANDER ONE: Oh, what a clever blow!

BYSTANDER TWO: Down upon the pavement!!

BYSTANDER THREE: Give him a little air –

BYSTANDER FOUR: Air? he don't deserve it.

ALL: Oh no he doesn't!!

BYSTANDER ONE: Where's the gentleman –

BYSTANDER TWO: Here's the gentleman –

MR BROWNLOW pushes through the crowd.

POLICEMAN ONE: Is this the boy sir?

MR BROWNLOW: Yes – Yes I'm afraid it is the boy.

BYSTANDERS: Afraid! – that's a good'un… (*Et cetera muttering and murmuring.*)

MR BROWNLOW: I think he's hurt himself –

BYSTANDER THREE: I did that sir. Cut my knuckles on his mouth I did. I stopped him.

MR BROWNLOW: Can you get up –

OLIVER: It wasn't me. It was two other boys.

ALL: Oh no it wasn't!!

They grab him.

MR BROWNLOW: Don't hurt him!

ALL: Oh no, we won't!! Two, three, four:

A Short Violent Song

For when a crime's suspected
The Law most clearly states
The job of dispensing Justice
Is the Magistrates.

During the above the BYSTANDERS, with indecent haste, set up a bench, dock etc, and create the next.

TABLEAU

Mr Fang The Police Magistrate.

Scene Nine

Treats of Mr Fang, the police magistrate, and furnishes a slight specimen of his mode of administering justice

The Renowned MR FANG is drunk.

BANG!! (Gavel.)

Jump cut into:

MR BROWNLOW: I am the party that was robbed; but I am not at all sure this boy actually took the handkerchief, and I – I would rather not press charges –

MR FANG: Who are you?

MR BROWNLOW: (*Offering his card.*) My name, sir, – my name sir is Mr Brownlow –

MR FANG: Officer, what's this fellow charged with?

POLICEMAN: He's –

MR BROWNLOW: Sir, I must –

MR FANG: (*Bang.*) Silence in Court!

MR BROWNLOW: I was standing at a bookstall –

MR FANG: (*Bang. Bang.*) Are there any witnesses?

POLICEMAN: None, your worship.

MR BROWNLOW: I did Sir see this boy running away – but I fear that he is very ill –

MR FANG: Boy? What boy? Officer, what's his name? What, what?

OLIVER tries to speak but can't.

POLICEMAN: Says his name's Tom White, your worship.

MR FANG: Has he any parents?

OLIVER tries to speak but can't.

POLICEMAN: Died in his infancy, he says, your honour.

MR FANG: Stuff and Nonsense! (*Bang.*)

MR BROWNLOW: The boy really is ill your worship –

MR FANG: Three months!! (*Bang.*) Hard labour… (*Bang.*)

Mixed dismay and approval from the crowd as OLIVER faints.
A LAST MINUTE WITNESS enters.

LAST MINUTE WITNESS: Stop! Stop! For heaven's sake
stop a moment!!

MR FANG: What is this! Clear the Court!!

LAST MINUTE WITNESS: I demand to speak! Mr Fang,
your worship sir, you must hear me!!

MR FANG: Well, what have you got to say.

LAST MINUTE WITNESS: I swear –

COURT: He swears!!

LAST MINUTE WITNESS: (*Sing.*) **By Almighty God, that
the evidence I shall give, shall be the Truth – the
whole Truth – and nothing but the Truth – so help me
God.**

Applause.

I saw it done sir; the robbery…

MR FANG: Yes!

LAST MINUTE WITNESS: …was committed…

MR FANG: Yes!

LAST MINUTE WITNESS: By two other boys!!

THE ENTIRE COURTROOM: Oh!

They all turn and stare at MR BROWNLOW.

MR FANG: …Sir, that book –

MR BROWNLOW: Sir.

MR FANG: The book you were reading when the incident
took place –

MR BROWNLOW: Yes.

MR FANG: The very book you have now in your hand –

MR BROWNLOW: Sir?

MR FANG: …Is it paid for?

MR BROWNLOW: Dear me, I forgot all about that.

MR FANG: (*Bang.*) A nice class of person to prefer a charge against a poor innocent boy!! You may think yourself very fortunate, sir, having obtained possession of that book under very suspicious and unfortunate circumstances, that the Law declines to prosecute. The boy…is…discharged. (*Bang. Bang.*) Clear the Court!! Clear the Court!! Officer!!

The COURT melts away leaving MR BROWNLOW alone with the perplexing problem of a collapsed and seriously ill boy. MR BROWNLOW takes OLIVER in his arms. As he does, the COMPANY just pause on their exits and see this happen.

Then, MR BROWNLOW takes OLIVER away…

CHARLEY: (*Because he thinks this is the end of the story.*) …Aaaaah! Altogether now, aaaaah…

DODGER: Hold your noise.

CHARLEY: Ha ha ha.

DODGER: Do you want to get grabbed, stupid. What'll Fagin say?

CHARLEY: What?

DODGER: Yes, what?

CHARLEY: What d'you mean…

Enter FAGIN.

FAGIN: Why's there only two of you? Where's the third? Where's Oliver? Where's the boy!!! Speak, or I'll throttle you. The boy.

DODGER: The traps got him – and that's about all of it.

FAGIN: So where is he now.

DODGER: Some crib in Pentonville. I heard the instructions to the coachman.

FAGIN: Pentonville, my dear?

DODGER: Up Saffron Hill, right, Exmouth Street, back of Sadlers Wells, cross the Angel… Pentonville…

A sign goes up – PENTONVILLE – and without them leaving the stage we crossfade to –

Scene Ten

In which Oliver is taken better care of than he ever was before

MR BROWNLOW's house. As OLIVER sleeps, ROSE BROWNLOW reads from the book; as if reading him to sleep.

ROSE: And so the boy fell into that deep tranquil sleep which ease from recent suffering alone imparts; that calm and restful sleep which it is death to wake from. Who, if it were death, would be roused again to all the struggles and turmoils of life? To all its present cares, to its anxieties for the future?

She closes the book. There is a gentle tap at the door – everything in Pentonville is very quiet. MR BROWNLOW comes and stands with her watching over him.

MR BROWNLOW: Is he any better my dear?

ROSE: Still weak, Father.

MR BROWNLOW: Rose, there is something in this boy's face – Can he be innocent, do you think? Where have I seen something like that look before?

ROSE: Before, Father?

MR BROWNLOW: No, no…no; it must be imagination…

ROSE: Poor boy.

ROSE strokes OLIVER's hair; he wakes up with a start; then suddenly throws his arms about ROSE's neck – he was dreaming of his Mother when he woke up.

There – there – you must be very quiet or you will be ill again. You have been very bad. Lie down.

MR BROWNLOW: Tom; Tom, my name is Mr Brownlow, and this is my house; how do you feel?

OLIVER: My name's Oliver.

MR BROWNLOW: Oliver? Oliver what? Oliver White, eh?

OLIVER: Oliver Twist.

MR BROWNLOW: What made you tell the magistrate your name was White?

OLIVER: I never did.

MR BROWNLOW: Some mistake, I expect. (*ROSE indicates gently that he should let the boy rest.*) Well well; you must sleep, young man, sleep.

OLIVER: Yes sir.

MR BROWNLOW: See if the boy will take some nourishment Rose.

MR BROWNLOW leaves, troubled.

OLIVER: Is he angry with me?

ROSE: No, Oliver, he's not angry…

OLIVER: Does Mr Brownlow have any children?

ROSE: Yes, he does. A daughter, Rose – which is my name.

OLIVER: Rose.

ROSE: And – and he once had another daughter, who died.

OLIVER: What was her name?

ROSE: Be quiet now, and when you've slept I'll fetch you something to eat. Would you like something to eat?

OLIVER: Yes please.

ROSE: Good boy.

She tucks him up. Exit ROSE; meanwhile, MR BROWNLOW and MR GRIMWIG cross, in mid-conversation.

MR GRIMWIG: A boy?

MR BROWNLOW: An orphan boy, Mr Grimwig.

MR GRIMWIG: And does your housekeeper count the plate at night, Brownlow – because if she doesn't find a tablespoon or two missing one sunshiny morning, I'll be content to eat my own head – I feel most strongly on this subject sir –

MR BROWNLOW: What subject?

MR GRIMWIG: Boys, sir; yes, Sir; I'll eat my head, if –

MR BROWNLOW: We shall see –

MR GRIMWIG: We shall. Friend of mine had a boy, a nice boy they called him, but he was a horrid boy, appetite of a wolf. This boy of yours – I'll eat my head if he's not a bad one. Who is he, eh Brownlow? Who is he…?

On this ominous line BILL SIKES appears; MR BROWNLOW follows MR GRIMWIG, troubled, off, and we are back with:

FAGIN: He must be found before he blabs – Charley, do nothing but skulk about, till you bring home news of him – we must know where he is –

FAGIN grabs the DODGER.

I trusted you!!

DODGER: Let go of me!

He slips out of his coat to escape and defends himself with the toasting-fork. At the top of this action, suddenly, just as FAGIN is about to land one on him:

BILL: What's it all about, eh, Fagin? What are you up to, you covetous, avaricious, insatiable old…fence? I wonder they don't murder you; I would if I was them.

FAGIN: Mr Sikes.

BILL. You know my name.

FAGIN: Well…well then – Bill. It's that I'm afraid, you see, Bill, afraid that the boy may say something which will get us into trouble.

BILL: You're blowed upon, incher, Fagin.

FAGIN: And I'm afraid, you see, I'm afraid that, if the game was up with us, it might be up with a good many more, and that it would come out rather worse for you than it would for me, Bill, my dear.

Pause.

He hasn't peached so far, but he must be taken care of. He must be got hold of, somehow.

NANCY turns up.

Ah the very thing; Nancy will go and see if she can fetch him for us; won't you, my dear.

NANCY: Wheres?

FAGIN: Just up to Pentonville. What do you say.

NANCY: That it won't do, so it's no use trying it on.

BILL: What do you mean by that?

NANCY: What I say, Bill.

BILL: Nobody up there knows anything about you.

NANCY: And I don't want 'em to either, so it's rather more no than yes with me, Bill.

BILL: She'll go Fagin.

NANCY: No she won't Fagin.

BILL: Yes she will Fagin –

BILL thumps or threatens to thump NANCY in the face; we realise from her reaction that he beats her regularly. Still, she answers back.

NANCY: Wherever that child is, he's better there, than here, among us.

FAGIN: Ah!

Dodger! – (*The DODGER brings him bits of drag to dress NANCY for her mission.*) we mustn't have you recognised, must we Nance – there – very good – very good indeed; very…respectable. Very real and genu-ine.

NANCY has transformed herself into a parody of a respectable girl; she flirts with BILL.

NANCY: Oh, my brother! Oh my poor dear sweet innocent little brother, what has become of him? Tell me, what has been done with the little darling – where can he be gentlemen? Where can he be?

FAGIN: What a clever girl you are Nancy.

BILL: Here's her health, and wishing they was all like her.

FAGIN: I must have him found you see; and I trust you, Nancy – you and the Artful, for everything. Get on the scent, find him, and when you've nabbed him, bring him to the other gaff. Find him, that's all. I shall know what to do next.

He has ushered NANCY out.

We may stop his windpipe yet.

Everybody; Morrice!

Everyone scarpers, FAGIN takes his treasure box and scarpers too.

Meanwhile, back in Pentonville…

We see OLIVER standing neat and clean in a beautiful set of new middle-class clothes given him by MR BROWNLOW; OLIVER is nervous – he has been summoned for an interview; MR GRIMWIG is there as a witness – and, MR BROWNLOW hopes, to be proved wrong about OLIVER…

MR BROWNLOW: Oliver –

OLIVER: Don't tell me you are going to send me away Sir. Please. Don't send me back.

MR BROWNLOW: You need not be afraid of that – unless you give me cause.

I have been deceived, before – once, most particularly – in those I have trusted, and loved; but you, Oliver, I feel strongly disposed to trust. Indeed I find myself more interested in your behalf that I can well account for.

Oliver, I particularly wish for these books to be returned to the bookseller tonight. Will you deliver them safely for me?

OLIVER: Yes sir; I'll run all the way.

MR BROWNLOW: You are to say that you have brought the books back, and you have come to pay the four pound ten I owe. This, is a five pound note, so you will have to bring me back ten shillings change.

OLIVER: Ten shillings.

MR BROWNLOW: Good boy.

MR BROWNLOW opens the door and OLIVER runs off…free…

MR GRIMWIG: You really expect him to come back, don't you?

MR BROWNLOW: Don't you?

MR GRIMWIG: The boy has a new suit of clothes on his back, a set of valuable books under his arm, and a five pound note in his pocket. If ever that boy returns to this house, sir…; I'll eat my head – oh… (*Seeing MR BROWNLOW has gone, he exits.*)

OLIVER runs back on – he is a little bit lost – looking for the bookshop – we see him alone on an empty stage for the very first time…

Scene Eleven

Showing how very fond of Oliver Twist Bill and Miss Nancy were

NANCY enters solo; when she gets OLIVER, the COMPANY (i.e. BYSTANDERS plus DODGER, CHARLEY, TOBY, TOM) enters in response one by one by ominous one, they come out of the walls like malevolent rats, sealing every escape route.

NANCY: (*Works the house.*) Oh my brother! My poor, dear, sweet, innocent little brother! What has become of him! Where have they taken him gentlemen etc etc –

Oh my gracious I've found him!!!!! Oh! Oliver, Oliver! Oh you naughty boy, to make me suffer sich distress on your account! Come home, dear, come home. Oh I've found him. Oh thank gracious goodness heavins, I've found him. My little brother, my poor, dear, sweet, innocent little brother!

OLIVER: Let go of me!

NANCY: Oh! Oh! Oh you naughty boy! Oh!

BYSTANDER ONE: Shall I run for a doctor miss?

NANCY: Oh, no, no, never mind; I'm better now. Come home directly, you cruel boy.

BYSTANDER THREE: What's the matter here?

NANCY: Oh maam he ran away, from his parents, who are hardworking and respectable people – and went and joined a set of thieves and bad characters; and almost broke his mother's heart.

OLIVER: I haven't got a mother –

BYSTANDER TWO: You should go home, you little brute.

OLIVER: I'm an orphan, and I live in Pentonville!

NANCY: Oh listen to him how he braves it out.

OLIVER: Nancy!

NANCY: You see, he knows me!! Make him come home, there's good people, or he'll kill his dear mother.

BILL: Come home to your poor mother, you young dog.

OLIVER: I don't belong to them. I don't know who they are. Help me. Help!

BILL: I'll help you – books, eh? Been stealing books, 'ave you? Give 'em here –

BYSTANDER FOUR: You naughty, hardened little wretch.

And then OLIVER gets properly, realistically hit by BILL – an action to really raise the temperature before the interval – or, the action freezes the moment before the blow lands?

DODGER: That's right!! Two, three –

All BYSTANDERS sing.

A GLORIOUS END-OF-ACT SONG ABOUT HOW TO TREAT BAD CHILDREN.

ALL: **That's the only way to do it to be sure –**

OLIVER: **Help me, help!!**

ALL: **That's the only way to bring him to senses** – naughty boy!
**That's right, that's right, that's right,
Take him home to his poor mother –
It'll do him do him do him do him good!!
– Do Him Good!**

TABLEAU

OLIVER BEING FORCIBLY HELD IN THE BOSOM OF HIS NEW 'FAMILY'.

Then:

BILL: Come on!

Exit OLIVER struggling with his captors, as the DODGER picks up one of the stolen books and reads from it:

What could one poor child do? Darkness had set in; it was a low neighbourhood; no help was near; resistance was useless. If he had cried out, nobody would have heard; and if they had heard…who would have cared?

The interval curtain comes down.

ACT TWO

Scene Twelve

Which shows what became of Oliver Twist after he had been claimed by Nancy

As the curtain goes up, FAGIN, with DODGER, CHARLEY, TOM, and TOBY, OLIVER is dragged struggling into the room by BILL. NANCY with watching

TABLEAU

OLIVER CAPTIVE.

FAGIN: Delighted to see you looking so well, my dear. Why didn't you write, my dear, and say you were coming? We'd have got something warm for supper.

CHARLEY: Look at his togs, Fagin. Look at his togs.

TOM: Lovely cloth.

TOBY: Aint you the gentleman.

CHARLEY grabs OLIVER's books

CHARLEY: Beautiful writing, ain't it, Oliver?

OLIVER: Please – they'll think I stole them.

FAGIN: You're right, Oliver; they will. So, you wanted to get away from us, Oliver, did you? Eh?

Wanted to get assistance; wanted to call for the police; did you? We'll soon cure you of that.

We really think he's going to get badly beaten now, but NANCY intervenes.

NANCY: No! – let him be – or I'll put the mark on some of you –

FAGIN: Why, Nancy!

NANCY: You've got him back; isn't that enough?

BILL: Quiet!

NANCY: No, I won't be.

BILL: Keep quiet or I'll quiet you.

> You're a nice one, Nance, to take up the humane and gen-
> teel side of things. A pretty subject for the boy to have as
> his friend.

NANCY: God Almighty help me, I am!

> The boy's a thief; he's a thief, a liar, a devil, all that's bad,
> from this night forth. What more does he want?

FAGIN: That's right, my dear; he is.

> *NANCY goes to attack FAGIN but BILL seizes her by the
> wrists; BILL is too strong.*

BILL: Alright. She's alright now. Aren't you Nance.

NANCY: No she isn't. She isn't, Fagin. And don't you think it.

> *BILL releases NANCY and she walks out.*

FAGIN: Goodnight Bill.

BILL: Fagin. (*As he goes.*) What makes you take so much pains
about one chalk-faced kid, when there's fifty boys snoozing
about Covent Garden every night for you to pick and
choose from?

FAGIN: Because they're no use to me Bill. Their looks
convict 'em as soon as they get into trouble. But with this
boy, properly managed, I can do what I couldn't with
twenty of them. Goodnight, Bill.

> *Exit BILL.*

> Charley, Tom, Toby; bed.

As they exit; to OLIVER.

TOBY: You was brought up bad, see; brought up naughty –

TOM: Never knew a mother's love –

CHARLEY: He'll be the death of us, I know he will!

They've gone.

DODGER: We'll make something of him, won't we.

FAGIN: Dodger.

DODGER exit.

Ingratitude; a crying sin, Oliver.

Wilfully absenting yourself from the society of your anxious friends – endeavouring to escape, after so much trouble and expense had been incurred to procure your recovery – escape, from those who have fed you. Cherished you. Taken you in. Tch Tch Tch. Such ingratitude in one so young. I do hope, Oliver, I shall never be obliged to submit you to any unpleasantness, any unpleasant operation in consequence of your behaviour. There was one young person, one young boy, of my acquaintance, a most wrong-headed and treacherous young person, who, like you, evinced a desire to communicate with the police…and he, Oliver, unfortunately came to be hanged at the Old Bailey one morning. Which is a most disagreeable and uncomfortable end for a boy.

But if you was to keep quiet, Oliver, and apply yourself to the business, then I should say that you and I will be friends. Very select friends.

Family.

FAGIN shows the boy to the audience.

The boy has been brought up bad, you see… Of course it won't be easy to train him to the business. He's not like other boys…are you Oliver? Face like an angel…

Hundreds of pounds, this boys face is worth to me. And if I don't make something of him, somebody else will…

Up until now, I know, his heart hasn't been in it; I had nothing to frighten him with, you see- which you must always have, in the beginning, with a boy, or you labour in vain. But now, I have it… Once fill a boy's mind with the idea he's been a thief; and he's ours! Ours for life!; Now I have him in my toil – I shall slowly instill into his soul a poison which, I trust, will blacken it, and change its hue for ever…ha ha!

Oh! The suspense! The fearful, acute suspense of sitting idly by while the life of one so young is trembling in the balance; the desperate anxiety to be doing something, to lessen the danger; to relieve the destruction which you have no power to alleviate!! Ha!

You don't even know what a thief is, do you, Oliver.

OLIVER: I do sir. You're one.

FAGIN: I am. And so's Charley; so's Tom, so's Toby; so's the Dodger: so's Bill; so's Nancy. We all are. And now, Oliver, you are. A thief: a thief, a liar, a devil, all that's bad, from this night forth.

It's a jolly life. While it lasts. Come and sit by the fire.

OLIVER: Let me go.

FAGIN: I'd rather not. Come here. Come here.

He does.

Good boy.

Now go to sleep, Oliver.

He does…

A month with me, and he won't know what's good for him.

Like a parent leaving its child safely asleep again after they have woken up from a nightmare, he leaves.

Scene Thirteen

While Oliver lay sleeping

OLIVER sleeps.

And just when FAGIN thought he had total control of OLIVER, of the audience and of the story –

NANCY crosses the stage, anxious and thoughtful, thinking about OLIVER.

And, in a rhyming action, ROSE does the same.

NANCY exits.

MR GRIMWIG has entered.

MR GRIMWIG: (*To the audience.*) That boy was an impostor. A thorough-paced little villain, all his life. If they had taken my advice –

ROSE: People who don't know what children are shouldn't say anything about them Mr Grimwig.

MR GRIMWIG: Well, I'll eat my… (*To audience.*) An impostor – I knew it, all along.

He leaves. And ROSE, before leaving herself, has decided what to do next; she activates the mechanism by which a giant placard descends, concealing the sleeping boy. It reads:

FIVE GUINEAS
REWARD

A YOUNG BOY, NAMED OLIVER TWIST, WAS ENTICED, ON THURSDAY EVENING LAST, FROM HIS HOME, AT PENTONVILLE; AND HAS NOT SINCE BEEN HEARD OF. THE ABOVE REWARD WILL BE PAID TO ANY PERSON WHO WILL GIVE SUCH INFORMATION AS WILL LEAD TO THE DISCOVERY OF THE SAID OLIVER TWIST, OR TEND TO THROW ANY LIGHT UPON HIS HISTORY.

APPLY TO
MR BROWNLOW, 23 MYDDLETON TERRACE, PENTONVILLE.

Scene Fourteen

Which contains the substance of a pleasant conversation between Mr Bumble and a Lady

MR BUMBLE begins a lecture on the moral of the story so far; (please note, MR BUMBLE may be slightly drunk; and that MRS CORNEY is now MRS BUMBLE – yes, dear reader – she married him).

MR BUMBLE: Ahem. The sin and wickedness of the lower orders in this parish is a frightful thing. They is as brazen as alabaster, and if Parliament don't take their abominable courses under consideration, this country's ruined. Ruined. They're all in one story, gentlemen; the demogalization –

MRS BUMBLE: (*Having spotted an item in her newspaper.*) Oliver Twist!!

MR BUMBLE: Twist? Twist, my angel? A ill-conditioned, wicious, bad-disposed child. Out-dacious; of all the artful and designing orphans that I ever seed, the most bare-facedest.

MRS BUMBLE: (*Putting on her bonnet.*) You fool, read that.

MR BUMBLE: …Pentonville, my love?

MRS BUMBLE: (*Exiting.*) Are you going to sit snoring there all day?

MR BUMBLE: Certainly not, my dear, certainly not – I'm coming, my dear! Really, since our marriage, she is so very violent. Really I –

As he leaves, he hauls the placard up and out, revealing not OLIVER but NANCY in Pentoville, in ROSE's front parlour; she is holding a newspaper, in which she has seen the same advertisement.

Scene Fifteen

A strange interview

SERVANT: (*With attitude.*) Mr Brownlow's not here.

NANCY: I must see him.

SERVANT: Would you wait here a moment...Miss.

He exits. Pause. Enter ROSE.

ROSE: Tell me why you wish to see me.

NANCY: (*Looking at the fine room and at her clothes.*) Oh lady, if there was more lived like you, there'd be fewer like me, there would.

ROSE: Please sit down. If you are in poverty or affliction –

NANCY: Never speak kindly to a person till you knows them better, Miss. Is that door shut?

ROSE: Yes; why?

NANCY: Because I am about to put my life, and the lives of others, in your hands. I am the girl that dragged little Oliver away the night he left this house carrying them books.

ROSE: You!

NANCY: Me. One of them infamous creatures you've heard of, that lives among the thieves, and never from the moment her eyes opened on London has known any better.

ROSE: Where is he?

NANCY: He's safe. Safe as I can keep him.

ROSE: Why have you come here if you will not tell me where the child is?

NANCY: I have stolen away, from those as would surely murder me if they knew I was here, to tell you the boy's alive. And now… (*She looks at the room again.*) I must go back.

ROSE: Why must you go back?

NANCY: I wish to go back, lady.

ROSE: Why? If you were to repeat your information to –

NANCY: Because…because of things I can't tell to an innocent lady like you. Because there's one…someone… the most desperate of the lot: that I can't leave. No – can't leave him now, anyways, it's too late –

ROSE: It is never too late.

NANCY: Excuse me Miss: I'm expected.

She goes to leave.

ROSE: Bring me news of Oliver again – Where can I find you?

NANCY stops in the doorway.

NANCY: Will you promise me I shan't be watched or followed?

ROSE: I promise you.

NANCY: Every Sunday night, from eleven until the clock strikes twelve, I will walk on London Bridge. If I'm alive. (*She turns and goes.*)

ROSE: Stay – You will take some money –

NANCY: Not a penny. God bless you, Miss.

NANCY goes, and ROSE sinks into a chair, wondering if this extraordinary interview was more a dream than an actual occurrence, and endeavours to collect her wandering thoughts. As she dreams, DODGER, CHARLEY, TOM, TOBY enter the house, almost as if this was a burglary instead of a scene-change – ROSE and the parlour are cleared away – and the boys find OLIVER, still asleep, right where we left him.

TABLEAU

The Boys Loom Over His Sleeping Body.

This picture is broken by FAGIN entering.

Scene Sixteen

Wherein Oliver is delivered over to Mr Bill Sikes

When FAGIN catches them with OLIVER, the boys scarper; the DODGER lingers.

FAGIN: And you, Dodger.

The DODGER goes. FAGIN looks at the sleeping OLIVER.

He hums a lullaby as BILL looms out of the shadows.

NANCY also slips on, late, returning from her guilty errand, taking off her shawl.

BILL: Well if it isn't the devil with his great-coat on.

FAGIN: …ah, Bill. A cold night, and no mistake. About the job in Chertsey, Bill.

BILL: Wot about it?

FAGIN: Such plate Bill, such plate –

BILL: And barred up at night like it was in a jail.

FAGIN: What you want is a boy. And not a big one – Bill – (*Indicates NANCY eavesdropping.*)

NANCY: Go on Fagin, I knows what you're going to say.

FAGIN: Aren't you the clever one. He's just the size for a window – and well-trained; he'll do everything you want, Bill, he can't help himself. If you frighten him enough.

BILL: Listen, anything wrong about him and you won't see him alive again, Fagin. Think about that, before you hand him over.

FAGIN: Oh I have thought about it, Bill. We need him in the same boat as us –

NANCY: When. When's the job?

FAGIN: Ah, to be sure; when?

BILL: (*Considers.*) Night after tomorrow. Monday.

FAGIN: Good. There's no moon?

BILL: No.

FAGIN: And –

BILL: All arranged.

FAGIN: Good, Bill, good – Nancy, why don't you stop here, and bring the boy over later. Be sure to tell him Mr Sikes is a rough man, who thinks nothing of blood when his own is up; he must do what he's bid. He can read his books, till he's fetched.

FAGIN scrutinises NANCY. Exit BILL and FAGIN.

NANCY and the sleeping OLIVER.

NANCY: God forgive me I never thought of this.

OLIVER wakes up with a start.

OLIVER: Nancy – what is it? Are you ill?

NANCY: It's this damp dirty room I expect. (*She fetches his shoes.*) You're to go to Mr Sikes.

OLIVER: (*Afraid.*) What for?

NANCY: Listen; if I could help you, I would; but I can't. I have promised for you being quiet and good tonight, and you remember that; every word from you, is a blow for me. Give me your hand.

As OLIVER, terrified, eventually gives her his hand; a moment of contact between them; jump cut; enter BILL, dressed for the job, with his bag of housebreakers tools.

Here he is Bill.

BILL: Did he come quiet?

NANCY: Like a lamb.

BILL: Glad to hear it. Come 'ere, young'un. Now; do you know wot this is.

BILL gets out his gun.

OLIVER: Yes.

BILL: And wot a bullet is.

NANCY: Bill –

OLIVER: Yes sir.

BILL: Well… (*He puts the gun to OLIVER's temple.*) …if you speak a word when you're out with me, that bullet will be in your head without notice. Of course, if there's people nearby, I'll do the business with a crack on the head, which makes no noise, and is more genteel. So if you do make up your mind to speak, say your prayers first. D'ye hear me?

OLIVER: Yes sir.

BILL: Well then. Ready?

OLIVER: Yes sir.

CHARLEY and DODGER and TOBY and TOM are creeping on to spy. A bell tolls five. NANCY has put her scarf around OLIVER's neck. She kisses BILL.

BILL: What's the matter with you?

NANCY: Matter? Nothing.

BILL: What'you thinking of?

NANCY: Of all the number of nights as I've waited for you, Bill. Been patient for you. Five o'clock, you said; it's time.

OLIVER tries to catch NANCY's eye as BILL takes OLIVER away. The moment BILL is gone, NANCY paces the room. Her disquiet, and her decision to act. As NANCY is in anguish, in tense whispers:

CHARLEY: Where's Bill taking him?

TOM: Chertsey.

TOBY: Where?

DODGER: Chertsey – Bethnal Green, Finsbury Square, Smithfield, Holborn, Hyde Park Corner, Kensington, Hammersmith, Chiswick, Kew Bridge, Brentford, Shepperton…Chertsey. A night there and a night back, they should be back Tuesday. Wednesday…

TOBY: Where are they Dodger?

DODGER: Thursday Friday Saturday.

Sunday…

Sunday night –

Jump cut.

FAGIN has somehow loomed out of the shadows – it is as if he had been there somehow, watching her.

Nearly midnight…

The boys melt away; and NANCY, having got her clipping from the newspaper with MR BROWNLOW's address out of her pocket, quickly hides it.

It is one week later, and FAGIN, for the first time, is starting to lose his grip.

Scene Seventeen

The time arrives for Nancy to redeem her pledge to Rose (one week later)

FAGIN: Three quarters past eleven, Nance.

NANCY: I know the hour, Fagin.

FAGIN: – Well where is he? Where have they been a whole week? Where's the plate – and where's Oliver!!!!… where's the boy, eh, the poor leetle child…

NANCY: – I'm glad to have him away. The sight of him turns me against myself. And you.

FAGIN: Nancy…you're drunk my dear.

NANCY: Am I? I hope he's dead!

FAGIN: Listen to me, you drab; listen to me, who with six words can strangle Sikes as surely as if I had his throat between my fingers; if he comes back, and leaves that boy behind him, murder him himself if you would have him escape Jack Ketch. That boy…that boy that's worth hundreds of pounds to me – Am I to lose what chance threw in my way? Eh? Am I? Am I?… (*He checks himself and, after a short silence, changes his whole demeanour.*) Nancy, my dear! Don't mind me –

NANCY: I never do Fagin – least, not when I've been drinking.

Nearly midnight! – oh, I need a breath of air.

FAGIN: Where will you get that at this time of night?

NANCY: In the street.

FAGIN: Where will you go?

NANCY: Not far. Just for an hour.

FAGIN: But if Bill should return and find you gone –

NANCY: I know that, God help me.

FAGIN: What is it – Nancy – dear.

NANCY: What do you mean.

FAGIN: If he – if Bill is so hard with you (he's a brute, Nance, a brute-beast), why don't you…

NANCY: Well?

FAGIN: You have a friend in me, Nance; a staunch friend. If you ever want revenge on those that treat you like a dog – like a dog! – worse than a dog – you come to me. Come to me. You know me, Nance.

NANCY: I know you, Fagin. Goodnight.

NANCY goes. FAGIN summons the DODGER.

FAGIN: Dodger!! Tell me where she goes, who she sees, and what she says. Move!!

Exit FAGIN. Then:

THE DODGING OF NANCY.

NANCY reappears out on the street. She is suddenly stone cold sober.

NANCY sets off across London; down alleyways and along dirty pavements, through the night – with the DODGER shadowing her. She disappears though a doorway; then, unexpectedly, MRS and MR BUMBLE cross the stage. MR BUMBLE is checking the address in the newspaper.

MR BUMBLE: …23, my love. 23 Myddleton Terrace, Pentonville. Brownlow. Five Guineas.

Exit BUMBLES.

NANCY followed by the DODGER again.

Then:

The BUMBLES entering one way and MR BROWNLOW the other; we are back in Pentonville.

Scene Eighteen

Containing fresh discoveries

MR BROWNLOW is in some haste, because it is nearly time for Rose to take him to meet Nancy on the bridge.

He gives money to MRS BUMBLE, which she hands to MR BUMBLE to count.

MR BUMBLE: Well?

MRS BUMBLE: There; it's a locket. The girl was wearing it when she died. There's a name engraved on the inside – no surname, just –

MR BROWNLOW: Yes. I know the name. My god.

MRS BUMBLE: It's gold –- rich gold; it's my belief she must have been of good family.

MR BROWNLOW: Oh she was, madam. She was.

MRS BUMBLE: She was gone – the child was sickly – so I took it. What's to say?

MR BROWNLOW: Nothing. Except that once this boy – once…my lost daughter's child, my grandson, Oliver – once Oliver is found, and safe, and the whole sad story of this long-suppressed proof is out, I shall take care that neither of you is ever employed in a situation of trust again. You may leave the room.

MR BUMBLE: It was all Mrs Bumble, sir. She would do it.

MR BROWNLOW: That is no excuse. You were present – and indeed are the more guilty of the two, for the law, Sir, supposes that your wife acts under your direction. Rose!!

MR BROWNLOW exits to find ROSE. MRS BUMBLE has taken the money and left.

MR BUMBLE: If the law supposes that, the law is an ass. An idiot. If that's the eye of the law, the law is a bachelor, and the worst I wish the law is that his eye may be opened by experience. By experience.

He exits as NANCY reappears. She checks that she is not being followed.

The scene changes to London Bridge.

The bells chime midnight.

NANCY waits; she is just about to leave, when MR BROWNLOW and ROSE arrive.

Scene Nineteen

The appointment kept

NANCY: Not here – (*She leads them off the bridge and down the steps.*)

MR BROWNLOW: Why will you not speak to us where there is light?

NANCY: I told you before. I'm afraid.

MR BROWNLOW: Of what?

NANCY: I wish I knew…none of them suspects I'm here tonight –

MR BROWNLOW: Good. Now listen to me –

NANCY: Yes?

ROSE: Please Father –

MR BROWNLOW: My daughter has communicated to me what you told her a week since. I had my doubts whether you were to be relied upon, but now, this meeting kept, I firmly believe you are.

NANCY: I am.

MR BROWNLOW: You must deliver up those you know who are keeping the boy.

NANCY: I won't do it.

MR BROWNLOW: Tell me why?

NANCY: She knows. I'll not turn on them.

MR BROWNLOW: You will not?

NANCY: Never.

MR BROWNLOW: Then bring the boy to us; and they need never be brought to justice. Without your information they never can be.

NANCY: Have I your promise for that?

ROSE: You have mine.

NANCY: They would never learn how the boy came back to you?

ROSE: Never.

NANCY makes her decision.

NANCY: He's with Bill – with the man I told the young lady about before. I'll bring him next week. Next week, here on the bridge. At midnight. I must go home.

ROSE: (*Stopping her.*) Leave him. You must leave him.

NANCY: Home, lady. (*Going.*)

ROSE: At least take this purse. You have –

NANCY: What?

ROSE: Take it for my sake –

NANCY: No! I have not done this for money. At least let me have that. (*Going.*)

ROSE watches NANCY go.

MR BROWNLOW: Rose…

He takes her away, as…

The DODGER materialises…and we realise that he's heard all of this.

DODGER: Next week. Here on the bridge.

At midnight.

Midnight…very dark. Midnight in the palace, midnight in the cellar; midnight in the jail, midnight in the madhouse…midnight on the bridge.

A candle glows in the dark; FAGIN becomes visible, sitting, waiting…

Scene Twenty

Fatal Consequences

DODGER: – midnight on the bridge, next Sunday. That's what she said. Midnight, on the hour, ha ha.

FAGIN: Good boy, Dodger. Go to sleep.

Go to sleep, Dodger!

DODGER does as he is told.

Midnight, eh? The dead of night. Ah!!

He sits waiting in his lair, biting his long black nails in mortification, hatred, disappointment, fear – and a fierce and deadly rage. He hears a noise outside door.

At last. At last…

It is BILL, coming back filthy and exhausted from the burglary at Chertsey, with OLIVER and with the swag.

BILL: There. Take care of that. And do the most you can with it; it took a whole week to get…

He sees FAGIN staring at him.

What? What? Gone mad, have you?

FAGIN: I've got that to tell you, Bill, will make you mad.

BILL: Oh? Tell away – sharpish, or Nance'll think I'm lost.

FAGIN: Lost! She has pretty well settled that, in her own mind already.

BILL takes FAGIN by the collar.

BILL: Open your mouth and say wot you've got to say. Out with it, you thundering old –

FAGIN: Suppose, Bill, the Dodger, that's lying there –

BILL: Suppose he what –

FAGIN: Suppose that boy was to peach – to blow upon us all – suppose he was to do that – of his own fancy; not grabbed, trapped, tried, earwigged by the parson and brought to it on bread and water, but of his own fancy; to please his own taste. Suppose he did all that. What then?

BILL: I'd empty his skull.

FAGIN: What if I did it! I, that know so much, and could hang so many!

BILL: I don't know. Smash your head as if a loaded wagon had gone over it?

FAGIN: Would you Bill?

BILL: Try me.

FAGIN: And if it was Charley, or Tom, or –

BILL: I don't care who it was.

FAGIN goes and tries to wake up the DODGER.

FAGIN: Dodger. Dodger. Poor boy, he's tired. Tired with following her so long – following her, Bill.

BILL: What'd you mean?

FAGIN: Tell me that again Dodger. Just so Bill can hear.

DODGER: Tell you what?

FAGIN: That about – NANCY.

FAGIN holds BILL by the wrist.

You followed her.

DODGER: Yes.

FAGIN: To London Bridge.

DODGER: Yes.

FAGIN: Where she met two people.

DODGER: Yes she did.

FAGIN: A gentleman and a lady, who asked her to give up all her pals, which she did – and to tell them how they'd got the boy, which she did – did she not?

DODGER: All right.

FAGIN: And what did she say about the man, the man what keeps her.

DODGER: I told you.

FAGIN: Again. Tell it again.

DODGER: She said his name's Bill.

BILL: Let me go.

FAGIN: Bill, Bill. A word. Only a word.

BILL: Don't speak to me.

FAGIN: Bill you won't be – you won't be – too – violent – Bill. I mean, not too violent for safety.

The DODGER backs away in fear, and gets out. Before he leaves, he takes OLIVER with him so that he won't see the next bit.

BILL stays right there, and the next transition is done round him.

FAGIN creates the next.

TABLEAU

NANCY ASLEEP IN HER BED, DREAMING OF BILL COMING HOME.

He leaves.

Scene Twenty-One

A ghastly thing to look upon

BILL: Get up!

NANCY: It is you, Bill.

BILL: It is. Get up.

NANCY: Bill, why do you look like that at me?

I won't scream or cry – tell me what I have done.

BILL: You were watched.

NANCY: Bill, for god's sake. I have been true to you. We could leave this dreadful place, and lead better lives. Or never see each other no more. It is never too late –

BILL thinks about using his gun, then picks up the club FAGIN once tried to use on OLIVER, and then, with all the force that he can summon –

Freeze-frame, just before the killing begins –

TABLEAU

THE BLOODY DEATH OF POOR NANCY AT THE MURDEROUS HANDS OF BILL SIKES.

DODGER: Of all bad deeds that, under cover of the darkness, had been committed in London that night…

ROSE: …that was the worst…

ALL: The worst.

Sunlight begins to pour into the room.

BYSTANDER ONE: A dreadful murder, it was.

BYSTANDER TWO: Was it? Man or woman?

MR BROWNLOW: A woman.

BYSTANDER: He's gone to Birmingham, I heard –

MR GRIMWIG: They'll get him.

ROSE: Let noone talk of murderers escaping justice; every long minute will be an agony of fear.

MR BROWNLOW: The description's been published –

DODGER: Blood, everywhere.

EVERYONE: Blood –

DODGER: – even on his feet –

EVERYONE: – blood.

The COMPANY exits, leaving DODGER to give a solo turn.

The Dodger's Second Patter Number

DODGER: So I'll tell you what he needs – I'll tell you what Mr Bill Sikes needs at this point in the story – what he needs…is this. (*Produces a little bottle.*) This, being an invaluable and infallible composition guaranteed in the removing of all sorts of stains – spick, speck, spot or spatter – from crape, carpet, or clothes – and only one penny a dose – yes that's right one penny; wine stains, fruit-stains, beer-stains, water-stains, paint-stains, pitch stains, any kind of stains; they all come out at one rub with this invaluable and infallible composition.So say there's a gentleman has a stain on him, a dark stain, say on a gentleman's hat, jacket or on his shoes, say, this would be what he needs, whether as I say that stain is a wine-stain, or a fruitstain; a beer stain, or a water-stain, a paint stain, pitch stain, mud stain or, a *bloodstain* –

We cut to the darkness of –

Scene Twenty-Two

On Jacobs Island

DODGER joins the remnants of the gang; CHARLEY, TOM, TOBY and a filthy, terrified OLIVER.

DODGER: When was Fagin took then.

TOBY: Just at dinner-time. Charley and me made our lucky up the wash'ouse chimney, but they took him.

TOM: You should have seen the crowd of women Dodger. The officers had to get in a ring right round him or they'd have got him. He was all muddy and bleeding.

TOBY: Becky from the Red Lion went to see the body, to speak who it was, and went off mad.

CHARLEY: They took her to the hospital.

Pause.

TOM: Fagin'll swing, won't he.

DODGER: He's accessory. If they gets the trial on on Friday, he'll swing Monday.

Knocking downstairs.

Pause.

Knocking again.

CHARLEY: Who knocks like that.

TOM: That can't be him. He wouldn't come here.

TOBY: Maybe he done away with himself.

Knocking.

DODGER: We got to let him in.

He takes the candle and goes downstairs to the door.

TOM: Don't leave us in the dark.

He returns with BILL – face covered and dried blood all over his shirt.

BILL: Tonight's paper says that Fagin's took. Is it true, or a lie?

DODGER: True.

Silence.

BILL: Is – it – the body – is it buried?

They shake their heads.

Why isn't it? Wot do they keep such ugly things above the ground for? Eh? Charley? Charley –

CHARLEY: Don't come nearer me –

BILL: Don't you – don't you know me?

CHARLEY: I'm not afraid of him. If they come here after him, I'll give him up; I will. I tell you that at once. He can kill me for it if he likes, but I'll give him up. I'd give him up if he was to be boiled alive. Murder! Help! help me – Murder! He's in here! Here!

BILL has got CHARLEY down and got his knee on his throat. He is just about to –

When –

DODGER hears something outside –

DODGER: Bill! –

TOBY: Voices!!

BILL drops CHARLEY. The boys start the next spoken chorus.

TOM: Noises. Footsteps.

CHARLEY: He's in here. Break down the door!!!

DODGER: Voices

BILL: (*Has his gun out.*) Is that door downstairs fast?

DODGER: Lined with iron.

TOBY / TOM: Hundreds of voices.

BILL: And the windows?

Banging downstairs.

VOICES: Open up in the king's name!

DODGER: Yes and the windows.

Banging downstairs.

VOICES: In the King's name!

Banging continues under.

BILL: Damn them. Damn them!!

He grabs OLIVER.

Give me a rope – a long rope.

Banging becomes a rhythm and increases in volume.

Give me a rope or I shall do three more murders and kill myself. Oi, you!!

BILL gets his rope and takes OLIVER as hostage up onto the rooftops as… The COMPANY enter to augment the boys in this next chorus. This is very controlled and deadly and inexorable, as if they had all now turned against BILL and were using the narrative against him. Under this rhythmic text, we begin to hear the steady sound of a heartbeat, thumping, getting louder, panicking.

Spoken Chorus

HUE AND CRY

Some called for ladders:
Some called for hammers: (*Shout of* 'Sledge Hammers!!!')
Some ran for torches: (*Shout of* 'He's up on the rooftops!!!')
– Soon as they saw him, faces in windows –
Sashes were thrown up,bodily torn out –

It was impossible –
Trying to climb up,
– 'Officer, shoot him!'
– Hundreds of people…
'Why doesn't somebody set the house on Fire!! – '
Crushing and striving and panting with impatience just to
get a good look at him –
As if the entire city had poured its population out to curse
him –
' – Look!!'

MR BROWNLOW: I will give fifty pounds, fifty pounds, to
the man who takes him alive.

The COMPANY become very 'calm', as they tell us:

COMPANY: Bill Sikes, having made it onto the rooftops,
determined to make one last effort for his life.
He set his foot against the stack of a chimney –
Fastened one end of the rope tightly round it –
And by the aid of his hands and teeth, with the other, made
a strong running noose;
Planning to let himself down by the rope, and then cut it
with his knife, and then
Drop.
At the very instant when he brought the loop over his
head, previous to slipping it beneath his armpits,
At that very instant,
He lost his balance.
Staggering as if struck by lightning, he…tumbled.
The noose was round his neck.

We see BILL having his neck broken.

– He fell for five and thirty feet, there was a sudden jerk –
– tight as a bowstring! –
– a terrific convulsion of the limbs –
and there…he…hung.

BILL, his neck broken and his struggle over, is then lowered slowly down into an open grave-trap to the sound of a

Sung chorus:

What a fall…
What a smash…
You should have heard them groan…

'With what a noise the drop goes down! –
How suddenly they goes
From big strong men with the strength of ten
To a dangling heap of clothes.'

Just as they are about to close the trap door over him:

DODGER: Fagin? Yes, they did get the trial on on Friday:

BYSTANDERS: The gallery was packed –
The jurymen…considered –
The verdict…
Was…

They slam the trap closed:

ALL: GUILTY!!

As the trap is slammed shut, they reveal –

Scene Twenty-Three

Fagin's last night alive

FAGIN in his cell. There is a POLICEMAN there to ensure that the prisoner doesn't harm himself.

Having pronounced the verdict, the COMPANY leave him to his fate.

FAGIN is battered; his hands are bloodied with scratching at the walls, his head bandaged from having being assaulted by the crowd; he is wild-eyed and absolutely still. He relives the moment in the courtroom when he was about to be sentenced, when he became aware of everyone staring at him, and stared back. 'All looks were fixed upon one man, but in no one face, no, not one, could he read the slightest sympathy. They might as well have been of stone.'

FAGIN: (*To the JUDGE.*) …Guilty… Have I anything to say my lord? Only that I'm an old man – an old man. An old man…

(*To an imaginary woman who shouts from the gallery.*) Sssh!

(*He is told to stand to receive sentence.*) My lord; to be hanged by the…my lord, till I am…to be hanged by the neck till I am… 'With what a noise the drop goes down, how suddenly it goes…'

Light! – why don't you bring me a light.

'Solomon Grunday, tried on Friday, tonight is Sunday, gallows on Monday'… (*Under his breath FAGIN tries to pray, mixing the prayers with blasphemy; he beats himself, and rocks from side to side.*) Ah!…good boys, good boys, good dogs; clever dogs. Never peached. Never told the old parson what the gentleman… Never brought any awkward stories to light. And why would they, eh? Good dogs. Good boy, Charley, well done, and Tom, and Toby and…Dodger – and Oliver – Oliver – ha! ha! – good boy –

Good boy.

Good boy; face like an angel.

The POLICEMAN has unlocked the cell door MR BROWNLOW has entered.

POLICEMAN: This is not a sight for children, Sir.

MR BROWNLOW: (*Sotto voce.*) It is not indeed my friend; but the child has seen him in the full success of his villainy, and I think it well that he should also see him now.

POLICEMAN: This way.

OLIVER is brought into the cell.

FAGIN: (*Still hallucinating.*) And quite the gentleman, now, Oliver – quite the – take that boy away to bed.

POLICEMAN: (*Holding OLIVER's hand.*) Don't be alarmed.

FAGIN: Take him away to bed! Do you hear me? He's been the – he's – somehow the cause of all this.

POLICEMAN: Fagin.

FAGIN: That's me. An old man, my lord; a very old, old man – and it's a poor trade, and no thanks, but, still, I'm fond of seeing the young people about me, and I bear it all, I bear it all.

POLICEMAN: Here's somebody wants to see you.

FAGIN: (*Seeing him.*) Oliver! Come here. Come here. Good boy. Now; I want to talk to you my dear – I want to talk to you. But outside. Outside. Tell them I've gone to sleep – they'll believe you. You can get me out, you see, if you take me. A little burst of tears eh? – good, that'll help us on, good. Good boy. The door, first. Now, if I shake and tremble, when we pass the gallows, don't you mind, but press on, press on. Softly, but not so slow…faster. Faster!!

The POLICEMAN intervenes and disengages OLIVER from his grasp.

A parent being torn away from its child.

'Fagin struggled with the power of desperation, for an instant; and then sent up cry upon cry that penetrated even those massive walls'.

Strike them all dead. Dead! Dead! What right have they to butcher me?

OLIVER watches FAGIN being taken away into the dark.

MR BROWNLOW: Oliver –

OLIVER: It's alright sir.

I am not afraid.

Scene Twenty-Four

And last...

ROSE runs in to hug and kiss him; MR GRIMWIG watching.

MR BROWNLOW: You're a good boy Oliver.

ROSE: A good boy.

Throughout this last scene, the light of Heaven begins to pour down, creating a radiant final

TABLEAU

OF OLIVER WITH MR BOWNLOW AND ROSE.

The DODGER reappears with an apologetic cough to attract our attention; he has the book in his hands:

DODGER: The little that remains to relate, can be told in few and simple words;

They (*Indicating the trio.*) all lived – well, as nearly to happily, ever after, as ever can be in this changing world.

The other characters – at least, those of them who are still alive, return one by one:

MR BUMBLE: Is that little Oliver? Oh O-li-ver, if you know'd how I've been a grieving for you – Oh Mrs Bumble, when I see him a-standing here among ladies and gentlemen of the very affablest description! I always loved that boy, loved that boy as if he'd been my – my – my own grandfather. Master Oliver, do you remember –

MRS BUMBLE: No he doesn't.

Mr and Mrs Bumble, deprived of their situations, were reduced to great indigence and misery,

MR BUMBLE: – and finally became paupers in the very same workhouse in which they had once lorded it over others.

MR GRIMWIG: Mr Grimwig…having had quite serious thoughts of eating his head, did not, after all; but still contends that he was right, in the main, to doubt the boy, quite right.

CHARLEY: Charley Bates.

TOBY: …and Toby Crackit.

TOM: …and Mr Tom Chitling.

TOBY: appalled by Bill Sikes' crime, fell into a train of reflection whether an honest life was not, after all, best.

CHARLEY: Charley, arriving at the conclusion that it certainly was, turned his back on the scenes of the past. And is now living in Northamptonshire.

TOM: Tom –

TOBY: – and Toby, I'm afraid –

TOM: – were imprisoned, for fresh acts of fraud and knavery, and were transported. And what happened to you then, Dodger?

DODGER: Ah, the Dodger; the Dodger – sadly – as a result of his bringing-up, no doubt – having also fallen back into the old courses – and in consequece of a wery sad case of deformation of character involving a silver snuff box- the Dodger, that out and out young wagabond, was snitched, nabbed, lagged for a lifer, and, in prison… died – aaah –

And little Oliver…

Well…

(*He looks it up in the book.*) …Mr Brownlow adopted Oliver as his son. Let the tears which fell then, and the broken words which were exchanged, be sacred. The child was safe, at last.

Final sung chorus:

COMPANY: **This tale's involved the best – and worst – shades of our natures;**
The ugliest – also, the loveliest – of all God's created creatures;
As we approach the conclusion of our task;
There is one final favour, ladies and gentleman, that we would now humbly ask;

That you remember, we have shown you nothing but what we said we would;
Namely, in little Oliver, the principle of Good;
Good, surviving, and triumphing at the last;
And Hope… Hope flourishing, where all hope was past.

The book is closed. The lights go out.

Curtain.

BIOGRAPHIES

NEIL BARTLETT – Adapter and Director

Oliver Twist is Neil Bartlett's twenty-first show at the Lyric Hammersmith since he became artistic director in 1994; others include productions of Wilde, Shakespeare, Shaw, Balzac, Somerset Maugham, Genet, Britten, Rattigan, Robin Maugham, Marivaux and Kleist, plus five Christmas shows. Neil has also made work at, amongst others, the Drill Hall, the ICA, the Vauxhall Tavern, the Derby Playhouse, the Royal Court, the National Theatre, and at the Goodman, Chicago. He was a founder-member of the music-theatre company Gloria, with whom he made thirteen new pieces of work including *Sarrasine*, *A Vision of Love Revealed in Sleep* and *Night after Night*.

RAE SMITH – Designer

Previous work at the Lyric Hammersmith includes *A Christmas Carol, The Prince of Homburg* (co-production with RSC) and *The Servant*. Other recent credits include *The Magic Flute* (Scottish Opera); *Cymbeline* (RSC); *Sherlock Holmes in Trouble*, *Port* and *A Midsummer Night's Dream* (Royal Exchange); *Henry VI* and *Mysertia* (RSC); *Closing Time*, *The Street of Crocodiles* and *The Visit* (RNT); *The Weir* (also Broadway / West End) and *Crazyblackmutha...* (Royal Court); *Juno and the Paycock* (Broadway / Donmar) and *Endgame* (Donmar). Future plans include: *A Midsummer Night's Dream* for La Monnaie in Brussels.
Website: www.rae-smith.co.uk

PAULE CONSTABLE – Lighting Designer

Previous work at the Lyric Hammersmith includes *Pericles*, *A Christmas Carol*, *The Prince of Homburg*, *The Servant* and *The Dispute*. Opera productions include *Die Zauberflote*, *Macbeth*, *Rigoletto* (ROH and BBC TV); *Agrippina* (Brussels and Paris) and *Fidelio* (New Zealand). Many productions for ENO including: *The Rape of Lucretia* (Adleburgh Festival and BBC TV); *La Boheme* and *Carmen* (Glyndebourne), as well as productions for Opera North, Scottish Opera and Welsh National Opera. Theatre productions at RNT include: *Play Without Words* (2003 Olivier Award Nomination). At the RSC: *Uncle Vanya* (Oliver Award Nomination). Numerous productions at the Royal Court including: *The Weir* and for Théatre de Complicité: *The Street of Crocodiles*.

GERARD MCBURNEY – Composer

Gerard McBurney studied composition and orchestration at the Moscow Conservatoire. His theatre music includes *The Phantom Violin* (1988) and *Out of a House Walked a Man* (1994) for Theatre de Complicite, the 'choreographic fantasy' for orchestra, *White Nights* (1992) for Kim Brandstrup and the English National Ballet, and music for his brother Simon McBurney's production (1997) of *The Caucasion Chalk Circle* at the Royal National Theatre in London. He has also collaborated with

Simon on a theatre piece about Shostakovich entitled *The Noise of Time* and most recently completed a theatre piece with Simon and Theatre de Complicite about Hector Berlioz. Gerard has made many arrangements and reconstructions of Shostakovich's music including a reorchestration commissioned by Pimlico Opera for dance-band of Shostakovich's 1958 musical comedy, *Moscow Cheryomushki* which was performed by Opera North and other companies worldwide. For the last two years he has been working as a consultant to the Halle Orchestra for whom he is also composing some short works for children's concerts. He provides consultancy support to the Bergen Festival and currently has three concert commissions underway.

SIMON DEACON – Musical Director

Previous work at the Lyric Hammersmith includes *Pericles* and *A Christmas Carol*. Simon originally trained as an actor and now works as a musician, composer / arranger, musical director, vocal-coach and teacher. A Fulbright Scholarship enabled Simon to study jazz composition at the Manhattan School of Music in New York, where he lived and worked for several years arranging and musical directing on and off-Broadway (including *The Taming of the Shrew*, starring Alison Janney for the Public Theater and *As You Like It*, starring Gwyneth Paltrow for the Williamstown Theatre Festival, composing (including a ballet for Jazz-Dance America) playing jazz and gospel music. Commissions as a composer have included a score for an adaptation of James Baldwin's novel *Giovanni's Room*, an opera, *Dreaming It Up* with playwright Noel Greig and a musical, *Fabula Urbis*, with writer Pat Cumper for Theatre Royal Stratford East.

STRUAN LESLIE – Movement Director

Trained at London Contemporary Dance School and The Naropa Institute, Colorado. Movement direction includes: *Slab Boys Trilogy: Solemn Mass for a Full Moon in Summer* (Traverse also BITE at the Barbican). *The Girl of Sand* (Almeida Opera); *Jephtha*, *Jenufa* (Welsh National Opera); *Ivanov*, *Oresteia* (National Theatre); *Katya Kabanova* (Geneva); *Attempts on Her Life* (Teatro Piccolo, Milan); *A Midsummer Night's Dream* (Regent's Park); *Iphigenia at Aulis* (Abbey Theatre); *Julius Caesar* (Young Vic / Japanese tour also as actor); *Endgame* (Donmar Warehouse); *Antigone* (TAG); *As You Like It*, *Cyrano de Bergerac* (RSC); *Easy Virtue* (Chichester). Directing work includes *The Holy Whore* and *SexyGenderBaby* devised for his own ensemble the*water*company, *Opera Cuts Carmen* (Welsh National Opera); *Mourning Becomes Electra*, *Serious Money* (ArtsEd London); *10,000 Broken Mirrors*, *Spinning* (Oval House) and *Song of Songs* (University of Illinois).

NICK MANNING – Sound Designer

Previous work at the Lyric Hammersmith includes *Pericles*, *Camille*, *A Christmas Carol*, *The Prince of Homburg*, *Aladdin*, *The Servant*, *Pinocchio* and *The White Devil*. Nick trained in stage management at The Central

School of Speech and Drama and is currently working as the Lyric Hammersmith's Sound Technician. Recent work includes *Excuses* (ATC); *Airsick* (The Bush); *Rabbit* (Frantic Assembly); *Great Expectations* (Bristol Old Vic); *Out of Our Heads* and *Susan & Janice* (ATC). Previously he worked at Derby Playhouse and the Gordon Craig Theatre where productions include *Cinderella*, *The Wizard of Oz* and *Godspell*.

NICHOLAS ASBURY

Nick first toured Europe with 'The Theatre of Public Works', as actor, musician, juggler and fire-breather. He co-founded Indent Theatre Co in 1995. He has appeared in *Pride and Prejudice* and *Dracula* (national tours); *The Deep Blue Sea*, *13 Rue de L'Amour* (Royal Theatre Northampton). He toured the world with *Henry V* and *Comedy of Errors* (Propeller / Watermill) then joined the RSC and appeared in *The Seagull* followed by the Olivier award-winning *Henry VI* and *Richard III* tetralogy in Stratford, America and London. He played Biff in *Death of a Salesman* (Compass / national tour). He then appeared in *Macbeth* in the West End. On television he has appeared in Dunkirk, *He Knew He Was Right*, *Romans in Britain*, *Doctors*, *Agony* and *Hetty Waintropp Investigates*. He was lead guitarist in Arnold (1990-95) and is still, just about, for Mookie; and as a jazz pianist has played the 606 club, Le Pont de La Tour, various festivals, and gin joints around London and Soho.

RYAN EARLY

Previous work at the Lyric Hammersmith includes Mable in *The Servant*. He most recently starred in *Troop* at the Etcetera Theatre. Ryan's theatre roles include Glen Garon in *One Life & Counting* (Bush Theatre C4); Dickon in *The Secret Garden* (Nottingham Playhouse); Wilf Crompton in *Spring and Port Wine* (West Yorkshire Playhouse); Starvling in *A Midsummer Night's Dream* and Decius in *The Golden Ass* (Shakespeare's Globe). TV includes Tom Nicholson in *Heartbeat*, *The Bill*, *The Dectective*. Film roles include Koko in *Beseme Mucho*, *The Slot* (C4) and for radio, Mathsman in *Mathsman* (BBC Radio 4) and Seymour in *Little Shop of Horrors* (Mercury).

MICHAEL FEAST

Previous work at the Lyric Hammersmith: Barratt in *The Servant*. Theatre includes: for the Royal National Theatre: Ted in *The Mentalists*, Genady in *The Forest*, Ariel in *The Tempest*, Foster in *No Man's Land*, Bobby in *American Buffalo*, Mayhew in *Dispatches*, Raymond in *Watch It Come Down*. For The Royal Shakespeare Co: Faust in *Faust 1 & 2*, The Duke in *Measure for Measure* and Beckett in *Murder in the Cathedral*. For the Royal Court Theatre: Card Player in *Prarie de Chien*, John in *The Shawl*, Joe Conran in *Ourselves Alone*, The Witch in *Elizabeth 1st*. For The Royal Exchange Theatre, Manchester: Subtle in *The Alchemist*, Billy Bigelow in *Carousel*, Roland Maule in *Present Laughter*. Henry Antrobus in *Skin of our Teeth*, Telyeghin in *Uncle Vanya*, Nick in *What the Butler Saw*. In the West End: Anthony Kersley QC in *The Accused* (Haymarket);

TOWER HAMLETS COLLEGE
Learning Centre
Poplar High Street
LONDON
E14 0AF

Renfield in *The Passion of Dracula* (Queen's) and Woof in the original cast of *Hair* (Shaftesbury). Lopakhin in *The Cherry Orchard* (English Touring Company); Macheath in *The Beggar's Opera* (Wilton's Music Hall); Narrator in Prokofiev's *Romeo and Juliet* (The Barbican Concert Hall); Fitzroy in *After Darwin* and Harold in *Clever Soldiers* (Hampstead Theatre Club); Verkhovensky in *The Possessed* (Almeida); Ivanov in *Every Good Boy Deserves Favour* (Royal Festival Hall); Jean in *Miss Julie* (Liverpool Playhouse); Mercutio in *Romeo and Juliet* (Shaw Theatre); Scrooge in *A Christmas Carol*, Nathan in *Nathan the Wise* and Dorn in *The Seagull* (Chichester Festival Theatre).

Television includes: *The Stephen Lawrence Case*, *Midsomer Murders*, *Touching Evil 1-3*, *Kavanagh QC*, *Miss Marple*, *A Caribbean Mystery*, *Underbelly*, *Resnick*, *Clarissa*, *Shadow of the Noose*, *Studio*, *Nightwatch*, *Blind Justice*, *Fields of Gold*, *State of Play*, *Boudicca*, and Christopher Wren in Peter Ackroyd's *London*.

Films include: *Long Time Dead*, *Young Blades*, *Sleepy Hollow*, *Velvet Goldmine*, *Prometheus*, *The Tribe*, *The Fool*, *McVicar*, *The Draughtsman's Contract* and *Brother Sun Sister Moon*.

Recent Radio: John Osborne in *The Charge of the Light Brigade* by John Osbourne, John in *Don't Look Now* by Daphne Du Maurier, Bloom in *From Here to Eternity*, Pio in *The Bridge Over the San Luis Rey* by Thornton Wilder, Nathan in *Nathan The Wise* by Lessing and Leontes in Shakespeare's *The Winter's Tale*.

NICHOLAS GOODE

Has an MA in Theatre Practices at Rose Bruford College. Credits include Valentine in *Arcadia*, Nicky in *The Vortex*, Mercutio in *Romeo and Juliet*, Ferdinand in *The Duchess of Malfi*, Hortensio in *The Taming of the Shrew* and Jean in *Miss Julie*. He has taught Music, English and Drama in both London and Nottingham. He has performed in various folk bands playing the violin and mandolin as well as singing in concerts in the Royal Albert Hall and Westminster Abbey where he was a chorister.

GREGOR HENDERSON-BEGG

Gregor graduated from East 15 Acting School in 2000 and went straight into a national tour of *The Hobbit*. More recent stage performances include Kay in *The Snow Queen* and Ruskin Splinter in the debut of Phillip Ridley's play – *Krindlekrax* at Birmingham Repertory Theatre. Gregor's television credits include *Lorna Doone*, *Nicholas Nickleby* and *Judge John Deed*. He also featured in the Oscar winning film *Gosford Park* in which he played Fred. He has recently finished filming *Ladies in Lavender*, directed by Charles Dance. This is Gregor's first appearance at the Lyric Hammersmith.

PAUL HUNTER

Previous work for the Lyric Hammersmith includes *I Can't Wake Up* (UK tour Told by An Idiot) and *Aladdin* (Told By An Idiot and Lyric

Hammersmith). Paul Hunter is a co-founder and Artistic Director of Told by An Idiot and has been involved in all of their work to date including most recently as a performer *Playing the Victim* (Royal Court Theatre). Other theatre includes *The Play What I Wrote* (Whyndhams Theatre). As a director *The Fireworkmakers Daughter* (Sheffield Crucible) and *Ordago* (Punto Fijo /Bilbao). Radio includes *My Family* and *Other Animals* (Radio 4). TV and Film includes *My Family*, *Hardware* and *Black Books*.

DEREK HUTCHINSON

Previous work for the Lyric Hammersmith includes *The Prince of Homburg*. He played The Messenger on Broadway recently in Deborah Warner's *Medea*. Extensive work in Rep includes *Elizabeth Rex* (Lord Cecil); *The Critic* (Sir Fretful Plagiary); *Greater Good*, *Villette*, *Way Upstream* (Alistair) and *Rebecca*. Dogberry in *Much Ado About Nothing* (Cheek by Jowl). For the RSC: *Julius Caesar*, *Measure for Measure*, *Taming of the Shrew* (Grumio); *Electra, Titus Andronicus* (Lucius); *The Churchill Play*, *The Family Reunion* and *A Warwickshire Testimony*. Work at the RNT includes: *King Lear* (Edgar); *Richard III* (Richmond); *Arcadia*, *Under Milk Wood* and *Napoli Milionaria*. TV includes *The Bill*, *London's Burning*, *Waiting*, *Chef*, *Crimewatch File*. Film: *The Cormorant*, *Iris*, *Being Julia* and *Compleat Female Stage Beauty*.

JORDAN METCALFE

Jordan has recently attained a place at Bristol University reading Drama and Film, and is currently studying for his A Levels. Theatre credits include: Jack (AKA Puck) in *The Dreaming* for National Youth Music Theatre (Edinburgh Festival, Guildford, Exeter Northcott and The Royal Opera House); and Nibs in *Peter Pan* (Royal Festival Hall, Christmas 2002/3). Television includes the BBC Series *Fungus the Bogeyman* playing Mould alongside Martin Clunes; and *The Queen's Nose* for the BBC, playing Jake.

OWEN SHARPE

Theatre credits include *She Stoops to Conquer*, *A Laughing Matter*, *The Cripple of Inishmaan* and *Pericles* at the National Theatre. *The Lieutenant of Inishmore*, *Jubliee*, *Shadows*, *Bartholomew Fair*, *This Lime Tree Bower* and *Madness in Valencia* at the RSC. *The Recruiting Officer* at the Garrick. *The Barbaric Comedies*, *Mrs Warren's Profession*, *Macbeth*, *Madigans Lock* and *A Thief of a Christmas* at the Abbey. *Brighton Beach Memoirs*, *Billy Liar* at Andrews Lane, *Jacko* at the Hawks Well, *Bugsy Malone* at Olympia and *Dear Jack* at the Ark. Films include *My Left Foot*, *Borstal Boys*, *Summer Ghost* and *Second Death*. This is Owen's first appearance at the Lyric Hammersmith.

KELLIE SHIRLEY

Kellie graduated from Webber Douglas in July 2002. Theatre credits include *Protection* (Soho Theatre); Catherine in *Boston Marriage*

(Octagon); *The Lying Kind* (Royal Court); *Chasing Dolphins* (Churchill Theatre) and *West Side Story* (Royal Albert Hall). Television credits include Kym in *The Office* (BBC1); *Jekyll and Hyde* (Working Title); *The Bill* (Pearson Television); *Silent Weapon* (BBC /Wall to Wall). Film includes Tina in *Wimbledon* (Working Title) released later this year, *Whacked* (Halgon Films); *Flush* (Freehand Productions) and the short film *Sticky* (Aurora Films). Radio includes *The Tall One* and *To Swallow* (BBC R4).

THOMAS WHEATLEY

Recent work in theatre includes Sam Walters's production of *The Road to Ruin* at the Orange Tree, Harold Pinter's *Celebration* at the Lincoln Center New York, Richard Eyre's *The Novice* at the Almeida, and with Nicolas Kent and Richard Norton-Taylor at the Tricycle, *Half the Picture*, *Nuremberg*, *Srebrenica*, *The Colour of Justice* and *Justifying War*. Work on film includes *Fields of Gold*, *Second Sight*, *Aquila*, *Bambino Mio*, *First and Last*, *Harry's Kingdom*, *The Living Daylights*, *The Singing Detective* and *Honest Decent and True*, along with episodes of *Auf Wiedersehen Pet*, *Foyle's War*, *Dangerfield*, *Taggart*, *Between the Lines* and *Heartbeat*.

LOUISE YATES

Previous work for the Lyric Hammersmith includes Neil Bartlett's *A Christmas Carol*. Recent work includes a new series of *Wire in the Blood* with Robson Greene and at the Battersea Art Centre *A Wing and a Prayer*, part of their successful *Scratch* series.
Theatre includes: *The Road to Ruin* and *A Kind of Alaska* at the Orange Tree, Richmond; *The Secret Rapture* at Salisbury Playhouse; *A Midsummer Night's Dream* at Exeter; *Of Mice and Men*, *Nervous Women*, *Hobson's Choice*, *My Mother Said I Never Should*, *Peter Pan* at Birmingham; *The Crucible* at West Yorkshire Playhouse. Television includes: *I'm Alan Partridge*, *Rik Mayall Presents*, *Reeves and Mortimer*, *The Bill*, *Coronation Street*, *Family Affairs*, *Brookside, London Bridge* and *Lloyd and Hill*.

BRIGID ZENGENI

Brigid trained at the Drama Centre London. Theatre includes: *Wide Sargasso Sea* (Citizens Theatre, Glasgow); *The Wedding* (Southwark Playhouse); *The Soul of Chi'en-nu Leaves Her Body* (Young Vic); *Phaedra* (Riverside Studios); *The Winters Tale* (RNT); *Twelfth Night* (RNT, national tour and New York); *Taming of the Shrew* (United States); *Madame de Sade* (Riverside Studios); *Bedroom Farce* (Frankfurt); *Mikado* and *Pirates of Penzance* (New Vic Theatre, Stoke); *Pericles* (national tour and Riverside Studios). TV includes: *William and Mary*, *The Cry*, *A Touch of Frost*, *In Defence*, *Dr Willoughby*, *Casualty*, *Holby City*, *Wycliffe*, *Holding the Baby*, *Beck* and *The Greatest Store on Earth*.